❧GRAND CHRISTMAS PANTOMIMES

By E. L. Blanchard

৩০৶

Tom Thumb
Aladdin
Beauty and the Beast
Jack in the Box
Cinderella

৩০৶

Classic Panto Series

T A P
Theatre Arts Press

Published from primary sources and other historical records.

For a complete list of titles visit

classicpantos.com

Printed in the United States of America
9 8 7 6 5 4 3 2

theatreartspress.com

❧Contents❧

Tom Thumb

Or

Merlin the Magician

And the

Good Fairies of the court of King Arthur

୬ଏଏ

(1861)

Tom Thumb was first produced at Her Majesty's Theatre, London, on December 26, 1861 with the following cast:

Gaffer Thumb.............................Mr. Forster

Goody Thumb..........................Mrs. Lindon

Merlin................................. Mr. Dixon

Tom Thumb............................Lillia Ross

Rosalia............................... Miss Mason

Tom.................................. Mr. Solderwll

Giant............................... Mr. Feefawfofum

King Arthur............................ A. St. Albyn

Huncammunca......................... Highbury Barnes

SCENE I

Interior of Gaffer Thumb's cottage, by sunset.

Large open window, through which is seen a village landscape--fireplace at side, with large kettle on fire—GAFFER THUMB discovered, busily occupied in chopping wood for firing—GOODY THUMB, arranging tea-things on table. After introductory Music, great Schoolboys are seen passing window, with satchels, etc. on their backs, as if returning from school for the holidays.

OPENING CHORUS

SCHOOLBOYS.
> BREAKING UP AND GOING AWAY--
> NO MORE SCHOOL FOR MANY A DAY!
> LONG LESSONS WON'T OUR TIME EMPLOY—
> HURRAH FOR THE HOLIDAYS, EVERY BOY!

> *(Shouts are heard gradually dying away in distance—Both GAFFER and GOODY THUMB suspend their occupation, at hearing shouts, and go to window and look out.)*

GOODY. Do you hear that? The boys are going home!
> School's over, and their holidays have come.
> Whils, Gaffer, we no blessed babe have had,
> To kiss when good, or soundly whip when bad.

> *(Another party of Schoolboys pass the window with their boxes, and the Chorus is resumed to send part of Air.)*

SCHOOLBOYS.
> OH! AIN'T IT PRIME TO THINK OF CAKE,
> AND ALL THE SPORT WE ARE GOING TO MAKE!
> LOTS OF EATING—LOTS OF FUN;
> HOORAY, BOYS, NOW EVERY ONE!

> *(Shouts as before.)*

GOODY. The merry rogues, they make my heart feel light;
> A laughing schoolboy is a pleasant sight.

GAFFER. Ah! Dame, I feel like you, our fate's distressing;
> A little one would be indeed a blessing.

> *(More Schoolboys pass, with hoop, footballs, bat and ball, and other toys—They peep in at the door.)*

FIRST BOY. Oh, look, here boys—here's Gaffer Thumb! Let's show

The good old folks some fun, before we go.
What do you say to have a jolly game?
Hop-scotch, or leap-frog—only give the name!

SECOND BOY. Trap-bat and ball—

THIRD BOY. Or chevy chase, I say.

SECOND BOY. My wig! for marbles here's a place to tiny.

FIRST BOY. I'll tell you what, we'll have a game at cricket,
And Gaffer's stumps we'll bowl at for the wicket.

(They pursue their games and mischievous pranks, till GAFFER and GOODY, with some difficulty, succeed in dislodging them. Exeunt boys— Old people breathless.)

GOODY. Oh, deary me!—what plagues boys are— its frightful!

GAFFER. Yet, dame, just now, you thought a child delightful.

GOODY. Well, if to us a boy should ever come,
I wouldn't have him bigger than my thumb.

(Peal of thunder and rain heard—GOODY sets tea-things.)

GOODY. Good gracious! here's a sudden shower; it pours—
How glad I am we are not out of doors.
There's one good thing, we are not out of tea;
I'll make a cosy cup for you and me.

(MERLIN appears at window, in cloak.)

MERLIN. Good people, prithee, from this precious pelter,
Give a poor traveler a minute's shelter.

GOODY. Ay, ay. Come in and welcome, my good man,
Though humble folks, we'll do the best we can.

(Enter MERLIN, through door, throwing off cloak over chair.)

MERLIN. Thank ye, good people, you are very good;
I've not forgot, Ma'rm, where the scraper stood.
It's a bad night to walk in, for a feller
Who can't afford to buy an umbrella

GOODY. Sit down and share our frugal meal, sir.

MERLIN. Thank ye!
Would you like to see a little hanky panky?
It's all I have to show for this reception.
Observe me, closely! There is no deception.
I am not like some wizards, so to speak—

No "preparatio"— no "mechanique."
I have no confederates— nothing to prepare.
No thing you see is here— and nothing there
I take this little cup in one hand, so—
Hey! presto— pass! you didn't see it go ?
> *(Taking tea-cup in hand and making it disappear.)*
Now, hocus pocus— hixtum stixtum— whack,
Hey jingo, presto, cockalorum Jack!
Look in the tea-pot— you can take it up—
I will not touch it— there you'll find the cup.

> *(GOODY astonished, looks in tea-pot, finds cup which she takes out. and, turning it over, a heavy purse, drops upon the stage.)*

GOODY. Well, so there is! good gracious me, how funny!

MERLIN. Observe, there's no deception—real money!

GOODY. Well, so there is; a purse full, I declare.

MERLIN. It is your own—take each an equal share.

GOODY. Good gracious, sir! you know a trick or two.

MERLIN. Ahem! why yes, I rather think I do.
I get my living by it, I may say;
You don't see such a conjurer everyday.

GOODY. I have half a mind to ask him. Gaffer, here,
(Aside.) I want to whisper to you— just come near.

GAFFER. What is it, dame?

GOODY. He's deaf— my only plan
Is, whispering it as loudly as I can.
I say, old Gaffer, do you think 'twould task him,
(Very loudly.) To make a little boy, if we should ask him?
Only a little one. He seems so kind,
To pop the question, I have half a mind.

GAFFER. Well thought of, dame; he can but answer, no!
I've half a mind myself, to try him— so.

GOODY. With your half mind, and my half mind, put to it,
I now have got the greatest mind to do it,
And so, here goes—

MERLIN. I know, dame, what you want.

GOODY. How wonderful!

MERLIN. And will your wishes grant.

Of evils you would choose the least, I see.
Bring me that book, and leave the rest to me;
Your lonely state shall promptly be relieved,

GOODY. The smallest gift most thankfully received.

(They bring him large book, labelled outside "The Child—Fairy Library" which he places on the table, and uses after the fashion of the Wizard of the North's Magic Album.)

MERLIN. This is a trick in which I want some aid.
Hey, jingo— don't be in the least afraid—
Pass hocus pocus— presto— popalorum—
And hixtum stixtum, jig, called cockalorum,
Appear, obedient to the wizard's spell.

(Music—His four Familiars appear.)

This is my magic album— mark it well—
Nothing beneath the table—nothing on it.
What have we here? It's something like a bonnet.

(Produces from book a bonnet which is given to GOODY.)

This for the lady—now for the good man.
A bran new hat— please to observe the bran—

(Products hat.)

A guinea pig— a birdcage— here's a goose;
A nice birch-rod, for which we'll find a use.
For, from this book, behold at last does come,
Your wish fulfilled, in Master Thomas Thumb

(Having produced the other articles as named, Tom Thumb is taken out taken off table.)

TOM. Hollo, papa! Ah! how d'ye do, mamma?
I've just come out, to ask you how you are.

GOODY. The little, tiddy, toddy, tiny dear.

TOM. Ain't I a whopper for a volunteer?
My name's Tom Thumb. Upon this simple fare,
My father feeds; his flock's I don't know where.
A frugal swain, who would increase his pelf,
And keep at home his only son, myself.
That's something like it—don't you always teach
A boy to show off in that kind of speech?
Well, what do you think of me, governor? I declare—
Oh! I say, isn't it rather cold up there?

Mamma, I've got a hint to give you—merely,
Put on your spectacles, if you'd see me clearly.
Well, what's the first adventure I'm to go on?
When am I going to be breeched, and so on?

GOODY. Oh, don't it do one good, to hear him prattle
It's pretty, little, dittle, tittle tattle?

TOM. I want alot of toys, and lots of things—
A box of soldiers who's the first that brings?
A rocking-horse and whip, to have a ride of it—
A drum to break, and find out what's inside of it.

MERLIN. I hope you are satisfied.

TOM. Mind, I am listening.

MERLIN. Now I must take him to the fairy christening.

TOM. Oh, are we going to see the fairies? Prime!
I wonder what they'll give me?

MERLIN. It is time!

(Waves his staff— GAFFER and GOODY disappear, and scene changes to—)

SCENE II

Rosewater Lake, and romantic haunt of the Fairies.

Fairies enter, preceded by ROSALIA, Queen of the Fairies.

SOLO and **CHORUS**.
HITHER, HITHER, FAIRIES, COME.
SHOWER GIFTS ON THOMAS THUMB;
GIVE HIM WELCOME TO YOUR THRONG
GREETING, BOTH IN DANCE AND SONG
THOMAS THUMB, WE CALL HIM!
LET NO HARM BEFALL HIM;
GUARD HIM WITH PROTECTING HAND.
HE WHO COMES FROM FAIRY-LAND.

(Tableau. Enter Merlin and Tom Thumb.)

MERLIN. This is the region where the fairies dwell;
Rosewater Lake—

TOM. In faith, it likes me well,
Trust me, good Merlin. Gramercy! odd's life!

Lake me no lakes!—I'll live here all my life!

MERLIN. Bless you, my child, you mustn't talk that way;
It's too much like the good old five-act play.
Your fairy godmothers will now bestow
Their gifts, to help you through the world below.

ROSALIA. I will endow him with a handsome mug—
A form at which none need their shoulders shrug.

FIRST FAIRY. I give him grace—

SECOND FAIRY. Good humour—

THIRD FAIRY. Fancy—

FOURTH FAIRY. Fun—

FIFTH FAIRY. Wit—

SIXTH FAIRY. Mischief— into which he's sure to run—

SEVENTH FAIRY. Activity, those dangers to escape,

EIGHTH FAIRY. And shrewdness, to assist him in a scrape.

ROSALIA. In short, though famous for his pranks and knavery,
The boy shall be forgiven for his bravery.
In home-made wine, with all the honours, thus—
Tom Thumb's good health! and so say all of us !

(The flowers of the foxglove serve as cups, from which they all drink. Tom Thumb ascends the foxglove-bank to return thanks.)

TOM. Unaccustom'd as I am to public speaking,
The honour you've conferred, without my seeking,
Makes me feel this— with compliments so rife,—
The proudest, happiest moment of my life,
If I sit down and yet my debt don't pay,
It is because I have nothing more to say;
But, feeling in return my thanks are due,
Allow me to observe— the same to you!
And add, to make my meaning still more clear,
A very many of em!

FAIRIES. Hear, hear, hear.

ROSALIA. Through mystic movements glide my fairy train,
Then, Merlin, see him safely home again.

GRAND BALLET

CHORUS.

HITHER, HITHER, HITHER, HITHER,
TRIP, FAIRIES, HITHER, TRIP, TRIP.
HERE COME AT OUR MYSTIC CALL,
YE TROOPS OF ELFINS, ONE AND ALL.
WITH EVERY STEP SO MUSICAL,
BY MORTALS SOFTLY HEARD,
WHO FANCY IN THEIR TWILIGHT HOUR
WE MOST CAN USE OUR MAGIC POWER.
COME, THEN, NOW THE LIGHT OF DAY
LEAVES NO REVEALING RAY;
YOU CAN ALL DANCE MERRILY HERE,
NO ONE NEAR, NONE TO FEAR.
TRIP AWAY, ELF AND FAY,
HERE TO STAY, TILL DAWN OF DAY,
MERRILY DANCING, HITHER ADVANCING, NOBODY GLANCING,
SEE, WE QUICKLY OBEY.
COME, COME AWAY, ERE THE STARS CEASE TO TWINKLE,
THESE ARE MOMENTS OF MIRTH FOR THE ELVES TO ENJOY.
TRIP AT OUR MYSTIC CALL,
YE TROOPS OF FAIRIES, ONE AND ALL,—
COME TO OUR ELFIN BALL,—
MERRILY DANCING, LIGHT-HEARTED CREATURES ARE WE,
NO MORTAL GLANCING, WATCHES OUR NIGHT'S REVELRY.

(Tableau—and scene changes to—)

SCENE III

Interior of cottage, as before.

Morning—Lively Pantomime Music.— GOODY THUMB comes on and sweeps floor, and arranges window, which now displays cakes and sweetmeats for sale.— GOODY, lifting up jar, labelled "Honey" finds Master Tom insides. As she puts buns and cakes out upon the table, Tom steals and eats them— at last, she runs to chastise him with a broom, and he shelters himself under a large saucepan-lid— whilst she puts the saucepan, having filled it with water, on the fire, which is seen in the fireplace.

GOODY. I wish that Master Tom would be more steady.
    It's time to get my good man's dinner ready.
        (Brings on table— prepares large basin, pudding-bay, eggs, flour, milk, which Tom observes from hiding-place.)

I little thought he'd play such pranks as these.

(Enter SCHOOLBOY, with large bag labelled "Cherry-stones.")

SCHOOLBOY. Penn'orth of sweet stuff, Goody, if you please.
There's no one here this bag to run away with;
These cherry-stones are what we are going to play with.

(TOM THUMB, having taken a lollipop unobserved, goes and hides himself in the bag, as soon as it is put down.)

GOODY. That's all I have left— my son himself supplies;
He eats up all my profits, worse than flies.
If I could only catch him now— deuce take him—
Wouldn't I trounce the little rogue, and shake him.

(SCHOOLBOY pays, and goes off with bag.)

GOODY. My saucepan's running out! I see, to-day,
Work for the tinker, when he comes this way.

(Begins to make the pudding. Enter TOM, through door, crying.)

TOM. Oh my! oh dear! I have been shaken sadly;
Those cherry-stones have bruised me very badly.
Didn't I frighten him, though, when I popped out?
I wonder what old Goody is about?

(Music.— Goody is stirring up in basin, when TOM gets on table, and, while her back is turned he sits looking into saucepan to see if the water is boiling, Tom, over reaching himself to taste the batter, tumbles into the basin and disappears. Goody hastily ties up basin in cloth, without observing him, and puts pudding into saucepan— visible movement going on in the cloth.)

GOODY. Another moment 'twould have tumbled out.
Lawks! bless the pudding! how it bobs about!
It jumps the more, the more it's getting hot;
Why one would think the deuce was in the pot!

(TINKER appears at window.)

TINKER. Work for the tinker, Ma'am?— scissors to mend?

GOODY. I find a leak here— just step in, my friend,
My saucepan runs— take it, you'll soon get through with it,
And pudding, too,— I'll have no more to do with it!

(GOODY takes off saucepan, when the pudding jumps out of it. Tinker at last succeeds in getting it into the bag over his shoulder, when he is observed to become uneasy under his burden.

GAFFER and BOYS enter, laugh at his perplexities as he goes off, and scene closes in upon picture.)

SCENE IV

Farmyard and rural landscape, with distant view of giant's castle.

Hedgerow and stile. Quick Music. TINKER rushes on, terrified, hastily throws the bag off his shoulder down by the hedgerow, and Tom appears from the inside.

TOM. I have been done to rags— I'm over boiled!
All my new clothes must be completely spoiled.
From getting in hot water this should stop me.
Wasn't it fun, though, when I made him drop me?

(Enter GOODY, with RED COW.)

GOODY. You little plague! why what have you been after?
My sides quite ache—

TOM. And my sides shake with laughter.
You've been and boiled me, if you'd know the worst.

GOODY. I'll pickle you, this time.

TOM. You must catch me first.

(TOM dodges GOODY about stage, and under the COW, but he is finally caught by her, and tied to a large thistle in hedgerow.)

GOODY. I'll have you safely,this time, anyhow,
Tied to a thistle, whilst I milk my cow.

(GOODY goes off, with COW.)

TOM. A pretty thing, to have a child and prison it;
One way of keeping children isn't it?
This thistle pricks my leg so, that I won't
Say this'll do, but rather, thistle, don't!
(Cow's head observed above him.)
What's this great thing, above me, I'm discerning?
It's a red lane, that hasn't any turning.

(COW swallows TOM and thistle. Music. GOODY enters, sees what has occurred, shrieks in horror, and, seizing staff, belabours the animal which causes the COW, being disturbed in its interior, to return TOM, and then disappear.)

TOM. Short profits— quick returns! A moment later,

15

I had found apartments of a roomy nature.
Notice to quit, in time, my stay abated,
And here's your lado' whacks, just waccinated.

GOODY. I'll fetch my basket—only wait a minute,
And safely home, my lad, I'll take you in it.

*(GOODY goes off for basket, and large CROW appears,
hovering above.)*

TOM. Here's fun! I like a lark, it cheers me so;
Crying won't do— I'm more inclined to crow.

*(The CROW flies down as TOM is sitting on a stile, tumbles
over, and is instantly seen ascending with him in his claws.
GOODY enters, calls on GOFFER and Purm Labourers, with
pitchforks, who, missing the crow, belabor one another, and so
go off.)*

SCENE V

Turrets and terrace of giant Hurlothrumbo's castle.

*Night. Large practicable window— window on level, looking out upon he
leads, and another projecting over river below. CROW crosses the stage
and leaves TOM on the leads.*

TOM. Well, as the crow flies, I have come some miles.
Where am I? On great Hurlothrumbo's tiles!
Not quite the place to tumble from, I know.
Deep is the river that runs far below.

(GIANT'S head, in night-cap appears at window.)

GIANT. I hear a fly buzz at my window-pane.

TOM. Hollo! the giant!

GIANT. There it is again.

TOM. He takes me for a fly— that's not the thing;
I'll quickly show him I have got a sting.
Just wait till you begin to yawn, my friend,
And down your throat a pill I mean to send.

*(GIANT yawns. TOM, having got a spiked railing, cautiously
approaches window, and tickles GIANT'S nose with it, which
produces a tremendous sneeze.)*

GIANT. Bother the gnats! how sharp they bite to-night.

TOM. A toothpick for you— full inside— good delight!

(TOM fixes the spike in the mouth, so as to prevent the jaws closing, and then tumbles down GIANT'S throat. Roar of GIANT, who withdraws his head, which is again seen projecting from the perspective window, and figure of TOM is seen cast forth into the river below. Closed in by—)

SCENE VI

Banqueting - hall, in the palace of king Arthur.

SERVANTS cross with various dishes—COOKS, SCULLIONS, and others, enter. Music—"When Good King Arthur Ruled This Land." Enter KING ARTHUR, and the Knights of the Round Table.

KING. My gallant knights, you must be sharply set.
　　What ho! my cook, is dinner ready yet ?

(COOK enters.)

COOK. A splendid salmon, sire, has just been caught,
　　For Arthur's royal Round Table, fit, in short.

KING. Produce it.

(COOK beckons on two ATTENDANTS, who bring a Salmon on large disks and place it before him. KING ARTHUR examines it with great satisfaction.)

KING. Salmon for our banquet boil,
　　Stop! half to-day— the rest for breakfast broil.

(The Salmon is being carried off, when, on second thoughts, the KING considers he had better make the division himself, for which purpose he proceeds to halve it by the sword.)

KING. There's something here my sword cannot cut through.

(TOM THUMB appears, out of the centre.)

TOM. Your Majesty, King Arthur, how d'ye do?

KING. Wonderful youth, that from a fish doth come!
　　I'll knight him. Kneel, and rise, Sir Thomas Thumb!
　　I've heard of you before— you have caused some sport.
　　My daughter—

(Enter HUNCAMUNCA, very tall and grotesque.)

TOM. Ha! 'tis time I came to court.

Permit me, rescued from a salmon's jaw,
At once to be your future son-in-law.
Out of a giant's mouth I make my claim,
The only good thing thus that ever came.

KING. Your valiant deeds demand some reparation,
But really this requires consideration.
The great art now, as modern statesmen view it.
Is when there's ought to do, how not to do it.
You are too small, the very least to say,
At present to direct your thoughts this way.
But in due time, in case we choose to doubt it.
We'll turn it over, and then— think about it.
  (TOM THUMB expresses regard to HUNCAMUNCA.)
Our appetite for dinner will not wait,
Bring us our bowl of furmenty, and straight.

  *(COOK and ATTENDANTS bring on very large bowl of
  furmenty.)*

TOM. What stuff is that? It smells uncommon nice;
I'll find out what it's made of in a trice.

  *(Manages to raise himself up a level with the bowl, and in trying
  to taste it, tumbles in and disappears.)*

KING. Ho! fish him out! I'd rather give a pound,
Than see Sir Thomas Thumb, our bold knight, drown'd.
Who here will show a subject's true devotion,
And plunge at once into this foaming ocean?
None! Cowards all! There's shame on every feature;
Be mine the arm to save a fellow-creature.

  *(KING, after cautiously blowing to get the contents cool, plunges
  his arm desperately into bowl, and brings TOM out in approved
  mock-heroic style.)*

KING. Saved! saved!

TOM. My life is to my sovereign due—

KING. I've saved my pound— a sovereign has saved you.

TOM. That's not bad stuff, I could have made a meal of it
When I was in it, I ate such a deal of it.—

KING. Safely bestowed, in future, Tom we'll see;
Our royal mousetrap his abode shall be.
Prepare the spacious residence we give,
In which Tom Thumb luxuriously shall live.

(Whilst the royal mouse trap is brought on at side, large enough for TOM to enter, the KING presents him with a small coin for a shield, and HUNCAMUNCA gives him a bodkin, from her back hair, for sword.)

KING. Of exercise he'll stand sometimes in need—
The last mouse caught shall be his fiery steed.

(TOM, who has entered mousetrap, comes out, riding a mouse, richly caparisoned.)

TOM. *(To HUNCAMUNCA.)* Fair lady, thus equipped behold a knight.
Who will defy all danger in the fight.
Each task imposed he'll make well worth his while.
If you reward him with but one sweet smile.
Come rat, come cat, with this good trusty blade
Thomas de Thumb of neither is afraid.

(Puts his charger through a variety of evolutions and then dashes off in true Astley's style.)

KING. Brave Thumb! though least, not last, among my knights;
No danger daunts him; see how fierce he fights,

(Sound of cats heard— TOM rushes in wounded and dismounted.)

TOM. I spoke too soon— ah me! that fatal thrust!
That outstretched claw— ah! well— what must be, must,
Curse on the treacherous spider there that Madame—
It was that tangled cobweb that betrayed me.
Though hale and stout, I fell a victim dire,
That trap suggesting— mews and goes entire.
Exit Tom Thumb— though very young my age is,
I leave my name to history's future pages.

(Falls off stage. QUEEN OF THE FAIRIES appears.)

QUEEN. Not so, although Tom Thumb here vanquish'd lies,
A good idea never wholly dies;
It is immortal, and Tom Thumb shall yet,
A hero be no child can e'er forget.
Leading of course to Tom's completer ecovery,
My fairy home will be the next discovery.
I always treat my favourites when I've missed 'em.
Upon the Fairy Home-eopathicsystem.

SCENE VII

The chameleon temple of the fairies.

Pantomime Characters discovered.

QUEEN. As for Tom Thumb, by just this little touch of him,
    As Harlequin we fairies can make much of him.
        (Changes TOM to Harlequin.)
    This maiden fair, to whom he did incline,
    Will be his sweetheart still, as Columbine.

    (Changes HUNCAMUNCA to Columbine. Enter MERLIN.)

MERLIN. To me, at least, allow a conjuror's boon—
    Yon see this cook— quick, pass! he's Pantaloon.
        (Changes COOK to Pantaloon.)
    King Arthur scarce can get much more renown,
    But still, we'll try it in the form of Clown.

    (Changes ARTHUR to Clown.)

QUEEN. Remember, ere you leave us, long ago,
    From Italy came the merry masque you show.
    Born in that sunny climate were Jong and dance,
    But English sunshine made their growth advance.
    That genial warmth will ripen us in time.
    Italian walls regain their Pantomime.

    (Comic Business Commences.)

E N D

ALADDIN

AND THE WONDERFUL LAMP

Or

Harlequin and the Flying Palace

❧

(1865)

Aladdin and the Wonderful Lamp was first presented at the Royal English Opera, Covent Garden, London, December 26, 1865 with the following cast:

Abanazar, the Great Wonder Worker..........W. H. Payne

Kazrac, his Dumb Slave.........................Fred Payne

Bo Ghee, Chief of the Efreets................... Mr. Lingahm

Aladdin, the Tailor's son.......................Rachel Sanger

Widow Ching-Ching............................. Charles Steyne

Princess Badroulbadour......................... Miss Elliston

Zobeide, her Principal Attendant...............Miss Farrell

Whack-Bang, Chief Officer of the Court...... Mr. Naylor

Genie of the Ring............................... Miss Dacre

Fairy of the Diamond...........................Lisa Weber

SCENE I

Abode of Abanazar, the African Magician.

Scene represents, a Romantic Cavern. Invisible chorus, which commences with the rising of curtain. An inner cavern at centre, screened by huge tiger skin, before which, KAZRAC the dumb Slave of Magician is seen stretched in slumber. As chorus continues, huge bats and enormous moths fly into cavern, and are seen hovering over the sleeper, whilst a large Owl appears flapping its wings over KAZRAC.

INVISIBLE CHORUS.
> WHEN ON EARTH FADES AWAY THE LAST GLIMMER OF LIGHT,
> WHEN THE MOUNTAINS ARE ROBED IN THE SHADOWS OF NIGHT,
> WHEN THE DAWN IS AFAR AND THE MIDNIGHT IS NEAR,
> WE SPIRITS OF DARKNESS TAKE FORM AND APPEAR.

> *(KAZRAC disturbed by the Bats that play about him, starts up, his terror and increase of alarm at seeing six Efreets or Spirits of Darkness, take the place of the Bats, and preserving in appearance their winged form. He rushes to centre for protection, and withdrawing curtain, discovers ABANAZAR studying a large volume inscribed with cabalistic characters. The Magician has a wand which he first employs to chastise KAZRAC, then to reduce the Spirits of obedience, which they express by bowing their heads, holding up their hands, and signifying the same in the unusual manner.)*

ABANAZAR. Dogs of the desert, am I thus requited?
These folks are friends of mine I've just invited.
I am their master—make them when I choose,
Shrink into their imaginary shoes.
My book!

> *(KAZRAC brings forward the Magic Volume on stand. ABANAZAR described round it a wide circle, through which the Efreets cannot pass.)*

I find some mightier Efreet must be near.

> *(They assent.)*

Abracadabara! let your chief appear.

> *(ABANAZAR ceremoniously touches with wand certain mystic characters in book. Fright of KAZRAC at innocation and appearances of BO GHEE, the great Efreet.)*

BO GHEE. Presumptuous man, who dares to summon me?

The might Djinn—the Efreet names Bo Ghee,
What is they will?

ABANAZAR. Great Djiin! this volume speaks
Of that, which yields to man whate'er he seeks,
Need I remark—of bashfulness no particle—
I'd be possessor of that useful article.

BO GHEE. There is a something of the kind you name,
But you can't get it.

ABANAZAR. Thank you all the same.

BO GHEE. Some friendless youth must first secure this prize,
All I can do is tell you where it lies.

ABANAZAR. Such information gladly I will pay for.

BO GHEE. You are mine already, but to make things safer,
This parchment sign—already sealed by fate;
A mortgage on your personal estate.

ABANAZAR. There!

(Signing book which disappears directly after.)

BO GHEE. Made the Genii—warranted unique—
A lamp conveys the power which you seek.

ABANAZAR. A lamp! not much in that, it seems to me.

BO GHEE. This lamp's a lamp most wonderful you see,
Where the Blue Mountains rise in far Cathay.
There one dark Cedar crumbles to decay;
Mark! where its shadow falls, then raise the stone,
The youth must seize the lamp, but 'tis your own.
This magic ring—the lamp is scarcely rarer—
Will from all peril safely guard the wearer.

(The ring is placed by the Efreet on wand, and it thus glides down the wand on to the finger of Magician.)

All that you need, you have at your finger's ends,
The Efreet's shadow hence your path attends.

(BO GHEE disappears, and KAZRAC, who has exhibited a great comic terror during the interview, is at last roused to a sense of the situation by the usual summary process. ABANAZAR signifies to KAZRAC they must prepare for departure; business of packing up; looking at map to trace route, etc. The Magician examines his wardrobe; puts on travelling dress. KAZRAC'S

*reluctance to follow; administration of contents of large bottle,
labeled "the Spirit Raiser." Magician concerned about safety of
his paraphernalia during his absence, so he writes out placard,
"Back in Five Minutes," and appends it to side of cavern.
Congratulates himself on his artfulness, and he then goes off
stimulating the flagging courage of KAZRAC with the sharp end
of his wand, as scene changes and discovers—)*

SCENE II

A Street in Canton, early morning.

*Scene stretches diagonally across stage, with shops continued into
perspective. Entrance gate, with Dome beyound, and inscription, "The
Royal Baths." Large shop conspicuous, Whang-Bang, late Mustafa, cheap
clothing mart and general outfitting establishment. On the other side of
the street, ranging obliquely, and with all the shops made out, are seen the
establishments of O.M, dealer in curiosities. Choo-Choo, the Canton
cheap dining rooms, bird's next soup not ready, the original house for
puppy puddings, etc. Hi-lo, cobbler. Twang-Twang, musical instrument
maker. Toff-ee, sweet stuff manufacturer. Chin-Chin, barber. Hi-Ho,
marriage register office. The shops are all being attuned to by the various
shopkeepers, who employ themselves dressing the windows, and
arranging their various goods. A troop of Chinese street boys come
swarming down the street, playing at different games which are continued
in front. Chinese games, kite flying, a Chinese top, leapfrog, etc. Then
pass the itinerant traders, seen in Chinese cities, such as the wine carrier,
the lantern seller, etc., and occasionally the promenades pause at the
shops to make purchases; the whole forming as lively a representation as
possible of a street in Canton. Two Chinese boys, who have been playing
at side, quarrel and come to front.*

1ST BOY. You don't know ho to play, put on your cap,
    I like Aladdin, he's the short of chap,
    If he was here—and it's quite time he came,
    Oh, wouldn't we just have a jolly game!

> *(General expression of sympathy with the remark. Then a joyous
> cry of "Aladdin," and ALADDIN, humbly attired, comes down
> the back to centre, bowling a Chinese hoop, and followed
> breathlessly by the anxious owner, a very small boy.)*

ALADDIN. There, take your hoop! I wonder now if boys,
    In days to come will use our Chinese toys.
    Five thousand years our lads have been contented,

With what their thoughtful forefathers invented.

1ST BOY. Now then Aladdin, come, let's have a game.

ALADDIN. Well, I'm your man, just give the thing a name.
Shall we make paper boats and each a cutter,
In the great Kennel have our grand Re-gutter?
Or play at tying pigtails in the street:
Or smoke Hi-lo, the cobbler, from his seat:
Or toss the pie-man, heads or tails you lose meant:
Or any other nice genteel amusement?

(The boys retire to consult.)

Air—"Aladdin's March"

ALADDIN.

OH MY! ALL THE NEIGHOURS CRY, THERE NEVER WAS A MERRY
    LAD, SO VERY BAD AS I,
ALL DAY, IT'S NOTHING BUT PLAY, AND IT SEEMS TO BE THE SORT
    OF THING AGREEING I MUST SAY;
WITH EMOTIONS, NOTIONS, I FORMED LONG AGO,
THE SHIRKING WORKING MADE ONE STRONG YOU KNOW.
AND PLAYING IN THE STREETS WITH ANY LAD ONE MEETS,
IS THE WAY UP IN PHILOSOPHY TO WISER GROW.
SO THIS HOW I SPEND MY TIME YOU SEE, JUST SO!
STUDYING HUMAN NATURE AS THROUGH LIFE I GO,
AND NEVER AS I'M MOVING I'LL DISDAIN FROM ANY JUVENILE,
TO LISTEN TO WHAT ARGUMENTS HE'S GOT TO SHOW.
ON LEMON DROPS, PEG TOPS, PITCH AND TOSS AND FIGHT A
    TARTAR,
RING-TAW, STICK JAW, PLUM DOUGH AND FLY THE GARTER,
OR TRY WHETHER WE MORE ADVANTAGE CAN SEE,
IN JUMP LITTLE WAGTAIL, ONE-TWO-THREE.
I'M OPEN TO A REASON IF I WITH THEN CAN AGREE,
NOT OFTEN DO YOU MEET WITH A PHILOSOPHER LIKE ME,
WHO STUDIES A VARIETY OF WHAT IS CALLED SOCIETY,
BUT ISN'T GROWING RICH UPON THE KNOWLEDGE AS YOU SEE.
THOUGH ONE WHO'S A TAILOR'S SON—A SOUL ABOVE A BUTTON
    HOLE HAS LONG AGO BEGUN
TO REAR, HERE, HOPES THAT APPEAR, ABOVE THE ASPIRATIONS
    WITH ARE PROPER TO MY SPHERE;
WITH HOLIDAYS, JOLLY DAYS, HOURS PASS MERRILY,
IN STRAYING, PLAYING, TIME NECESSARILY
QUICK WILL FLY, WITH THOSE WHO TRY

THE MERRY LITTLE GAME, THAT WE CALL "HI-SPI-HI,"
THEN RAMBLING AND SCRAMBLING ALL ABOUT WE TRY;
WHERE BIRD'S HAVE BUILT A LITTLE NEST A LITTLE EYE MAY SPY,
BUT THE NESTS WE NEVER THROW AWAY, BECAUSE YOU SEE WE
    KNOW A WAY,
TO SCOOP THEM INTO SOUP, WHICH IS A GREAT ECON-O-MY.

(Spoken.) And then how joyfully we go back to—
Lemon drops, peg tops, etc.

> *(At the end of song the boys seem to have decided on their game,
> and at the same time WIDOW CHING-CHING, with bundle
> and Chinese umbrella, enters, receiving the full impression of the
> first boy who dashes off in the game, whilst ALADDIN, conceals
> himself behind the other boys, who stand aloof at side.)*

1ST BOY. Here goes for Hi-spi-hi, I'm off like winkin!

WIDOW. A nice Hi-spi-hi you are I'm a thinking.
Drat the young scamp, it's such as you each day,
That into mischief lead my son astray.
But you are beneath him—he'd not mix with such,
A lad—*(spying him out)*—in there he is. I thought as much.

> *(WIDOW CHING-CHING chases ALADDIN out of the crowd
> of juveniles and belabours the boys with her umbrella till they go
> off, and leave her in centre with ALADDIN.)*

WIDOW. How can you thus my peace of mind destroy?
You lazy, tiresome, dear, delightful boy!

Air—"Chin A Ring A Ring Ting"

LINGERING A THIN THING HERE I FIND YOU,
WAGABOND'S A BAG O' BONES WE ALWAYS SEE,
TAG AND RAG AND BOBTAIL ALL BEHIND YOU,
WHEN YOU MIGHT RESPECTABLE LIKE ME BE.
NOTHING DO YOU THINK OF NOW BUT PLAYING,
SPOILING OF A TEMPER THAT ONCE MILD WAS STYLED;
NEVER WAS A LAD SO FOND OF STRAYING,
MAKING YOUR MAMA QUITE WILD, CHILD.
UP AND DOWN THE STREET OF CANTON, BENT ON
(DEEP DOG!) LEEP FROG, ALL DAY LONG.
NEVER ANY MESSAGE DO YOUT AKE YOU ARE SENT ON,
DON'T YOU THINK THIS SORT O' THING'S BEEN LONG, WRONG.
    (Sung a little slower.)
SURELY LIKE YOUR FATHER YOU MIGHT PLY YOUR NEEDLE,

TAKE A THREAD AND STITCH, STITCH LIKE A KING,
BUT ALL YOU SEEM TO CARE ABOUT'S TO WHEEDLE,
TWEEDLE, CHICKABIDDY!—LITTLE WIDDY CHIN-CHING.

WIDOW. *(Point to tailor's.)* There is a the shop your father used to keep,
Poor Mustafa he sold things on the cheap,
Until one day he sewed himself up neatly,
And so we go so-so sold up completely.
(Sobbing.)
I didn't know his worth whilst he was here,
But gone dear Mustafa must-have-a tear.

ALADDIN. Cheer up mama, I'm tiresome, well, you've hit it,
Fonder of play than work, true I admit it.
But I've a soul which spurns whate'er is real,
And longs to--you know what I mean, the ideal.
Throbbing with impulses fond, faithful, dutiful,
But seeking out the big, the bold, the beautiful!

WIDOW. Oh, he might write a book he might!

ALADDIN. Then please fancy it printed, words with great big B's—
And that it speaks of one Aladdin, who
Pined for a Princess that he never knew.

WIDOW. You make me quite forget, you great Tom Nobby,
You're but a child and I'm a poor old body.
(Shopkeepers re-appear. A tinkling bell rings at tailor's establishment.)
Hark! there's the bell, a summons none dare shirk,
And all from breakfast must get back to work.
Before I get *my* breakfast, I must take
Money for clothes they gave me out to make.
It's rather galling to one's feelings, this is,
Working for that house where one once was misses.

(Nine tailors' journeymen enter, and as they cross stage to go into shop, successively greet WIDOW with a respectful recognition, which is delightedly responded to by the WIDOW, who tries to arrack ALADDIN'S attention to it, but he is rapt in reverie.)

WIDOW. Only to think—

ALADDIN. Oh! region of delight!

WIDOW. I paid their wages every Saturday night,
Took off *his* ninepence.

ALADDIN. Right regains its own!

WIDOW. Fined him for buttons not being tightly sewn.

ALADDIN. Then having seen the Sultan with my mother—

WIDOW. Gave him one cuff for having spoiled another.

ALADDIN. I beat the Tartar and become the Prince!

WIDOW. How that young man has grown, and five years since:

ALADDIN. Having thus settled all known and unknown things--

WIDOW. It's time to make him settle for my own things.

> *(ALADDIN starts. The WIDOW finds he has been inattentive, but forgives him; and then she follows the last journeyman into shop.)*

ALADDIN. I shouldn't mind a mustiness, if I knew
For certain there would not be much to do;
If I had been a tailor, there's no doubt
I should have done what's called the "cutting out."
(Music of distant procession heard.)
The music of the future, I believe in,
Here sends a note some good news I perceive in.

> *(Music approaches nearer, and a double row of Chinese Police file down street. Chief Officer with staff.)*

CHIEF OFFICER. *(Reading scroll.)*
To all! This being the first day of the moon,
Also the sixteenth from the last monsoon,
The fair Princess Badroulbadour will visit
The Royal Baths--as you are aware this is it.
And as on Royalty no eye must drop,
All clear the streets and each shut up his shop.
By order of the Sultan Kiang Whang
Borriboo-Ghoola-Hi-Lo-Black Gang Chang.

ALADDIN. The fair Princess! How I should like a peep—
Ha! the trap door! I on the roof could creep,
Knowing each nook of our old habitation,
The tailor's son thus gains a lofty station.

> *(He exits. The shops are seen closed, and marked contrast of effect produced. Guards, etc. form a back, whilst the PRINCESS BADROULBADOUR and female attendants enter in procession, all veiled. PRINCESS borne in an palanquin by slaves, who, having placed palanquin in front, retire. The attendants form with*

their veils a complete gauzy screen at back. ZOBEIDE, chief of female attendants, in advance. As ALADDIN is seen climbing through roof, and peering over the shop front, the PRINCESS unveils, and a picturesque group is formed.)

ALADDIN. Fairest of faces, take my heart away!

PRINCESS. Who was it spoke? What did Zobeide say?
  (ZOBEIDE intimates there must be some mistake.)
  I really could have sworn some voice beseeched me,
  And rather liked the tone in which it reached me.
  It must have been but fancy. Ladies, rise!
  (Two attendants have assisted her to alight.)
  And here, secure from all intruding eyes,
  Take that mild exercise before ablution,
  So beneficial to the constitution.

GRAND BALLET

(At the conclusion of which, the PRINCESS and attendants proceed to the bath. Gong, and the scene regains its previous activity; the shops are re-opened, and ALADDIN re-appears.)

ALADDIN. That lovely Princess I am sure, some day
  It meant to be the future Mrs. A.

  (ABANAZAR and KAZRAC come slowly down the street, pretending to examine the wares of the shopkeepers. Enter WIDOW CHING-GHING from Tailor's, counting money.)

WIDOW. Let's see. There's three and four, which makes--dear me,
  I'm very bad at counting, four and three—

ALADDIN. Oh! what a glorious figure!

WIDOW. Very true for it,
  But recollect the work I had to do for it.

ALADDIN. The style so graceful!

WIDOW. All my own.

ALADDIN. Such taste!

WIDOW. There *was* a little.

ALADDIN. And then such a waist!

WIDOW. No, not a bit of waste; I used the stuff
  Up to the last—in fact, have scarce enough.

ALADDIN. Mother, my thoughts were--well, no matter what.

WIDOW. Here, look, Aladdin. This is what I've get
  For my week's work; it's very small, no doubt of it,
  Having to find my thread and needles out of it.
  But it's enough to get us—bless the lad!

  (ALADDIN shows emotion.)

ALADDIN. I never thought that I was half so bad.
  Oh! if I had the chance of some employ,
  You'd find the tailor's son a different boy.

WIDOW. Come to my arms! Her little pet she spoils.

ABANAZAR. *(Advancing, and aside.)* Work! yes, he shall! He can't
  escape my toils.
  This is the boy for me. *(Aloud.)* Madam, good day!

WIDOW. A stranger! Most polite one, I must say.

  *(Greetings exchanged with great ceremony, and imitated by
  KAZRAC and ALADDIN.)*

ABANAZAR. Would you be kindly good enough to tell
  Me, where the tailor, Mustafa, may dwell?

WIDOW. Mustafa--tailor--lives, alas! no more,
  But all he left behind, you are right before.
  Here is his only son, where *was* his shop.
  Here *is* his widow, and—

ABANAZAR. Good gracious! Stop!
  Stay! whilst I shed one tear my brother's loss over,
  There is the tear, and here is the philosopher.
  My brother's widow! Bless me, how do you do.
  That handsome youth my little nephew, too!
  How glad I am to see you. Let's embrace.
  I'm your rich uncle.

  (They shriek.)

WIDOW. Oh! if that's the case,
  Of course, Aladdin, nature's ties we feel.

  (General embrace.)

ALADDIN. Rich uncle! That embraces a great deal.

ABANAZAR. Poor Mustafa! he didn't, son or widdy,
  Leave you remarkably well off, mum, did he?
  (They acknowledge their poverty.)
  Well, I shall do the liberal. There's my purse.

Your name?

ALADDIN. Aladdin!

ABANAZAR. Might have had a worse.
Get the best clothes you can for ready cash on,
And let me see you in the latest fashion.
My servant will attend you. To be sure,
He doesn't speak, but then he *thinks* the more.

(*ALADDIN equally delighted with the purse and the proposal. KAZRAC anxious to warn the mother by signs, but the Magician keeps too vigilant a watch on his movements. ALADDIN thinks the Magician, and then, with KAZRAC, proudly enters the Outfitting Establishment.*)

WIDOW. Oh dear! good news I've not been used to latterly,
You haven't such a thing as "Sal volatile"
About you anywhere?

ABANAZAR. To raise the spirits,
Tincture of gold you'll find has equal merits.

(*Gives a purse to WIDOW, who is delighted. KAZRAC and ALADDIN return from shop, the latter smartly attired in everything new.*)

ALADDIN. This style of dress fits easier than the other.

WIDOW. He is a handsome boy. How like his mother.

ABANAZAR. (*Coaxingly.*) Will nevvy take a walk with Nunky Punky?

ALADDIN. Quite proud, old boy.

ABANAZAR. (*Aside.*) I'll "boy" him, the young monkey.

(*Business of ALADDIN taking leave of his mother, who most ceremoniously takes leave of ABANAZAR. KAZRAC in vain tries once more to express, by gesticulation, the danger of ALADDIN. The Street Boys come rushing to get ALADDIN to play with them; they observe his changed appearance. ALADDIN ask his supposed uncle to treat them. ABANAZAR'S reluctance and annoyance. At last he supplies the required money.*)

ALADDIN. Here boys, go in for sweet stuff, toy, and lantern;
Here's that will purchase half the shops in Canton.

(*The boys receive amongst them contests of purse. They spread themselves through the street, and return, with Toys, Paper*

Lanterns, and purchases of every kind, overwhelming
ABANAZAR with thanks, and dragging him into their games
against his inclination. The Magician is dragging ALADDIN
reluctantly away, followed by KAZRAC when the scene closes on
a bustling and excited group of the WIDOW, and the Children,
and the Shopkeepers, all singing—)

Song—"The Great Chinese Song of Jubilation"

WIDOW.
CHING A RING TA! FINGER RING PA!
MERRY GO MA! FUN, OH, LA!
YOU SEEM A PA, A GOOD DA, DA!
PICCOLO JAR, IN OP-E-RA!

ALADDIN. *(With football.)*
BANG TO SKI—KIEKITO HI!
PITTI WITS SHI—TI-MI-TRI,
IN A RING FLY—FATTI O-FI,
PERRIWIGS TIE—OL, LO-MAI HI.

CHORUS.
BANG! CHANG! NOW BUY
TIPPY, TREATI—SINGY SONGEE,
TEE—TI—TE—TUM
BIZZI BIZZI BEE.
BRING, SWING, STRING, THING,
FINY, MINY, LANKY, TANKY,
TIT—TAT—TOE—TEA
ALL GO TIM-BUC-TOO!
HUBABUBOO—ALL GO TOO,
CHIM—CHUM—CHOO.
LONG GONG--PITCH KEY WHO,
WHANG HE—SHAM DO—TRY BAMBOE,
STRIKI—KRIKI—OH KUM—BANG IT DO.

(Scene closes in on group.)

SCENE III

The Cedar Valley in the Blue Mountains.

Large cedar in decay at side. Enter KAZRAC with basket, ALADDIN
and ABANAZAR.

ALADDIN. Well uncle, thanks to legs being pretty strong,
And riding ostriches that flew along,
We have walked and ridden I think far enough.

ABANAZAR. Turn back! pshaw! pish! pood! stuff!

ALADDIN. This place looks gloomy.

ABANAZAR. Better will it fit
Our purpose. Let's enjoy ourselves at bit!
Kazrac, unpack the basket. Come, some wine!
A pic-nic in the mountains, ha! that's fine!

(Basket unpacked. Wine, etc. produced. ALADDIN and ABANAZAR sit down—the latter with bottle.)

ALADDIN. Would I were safe at home again! Dear me!
Please uncle, I think mother's waiting tea.

ABANAZAR. Tea! you're a spoon—

ALADDIN. In that remark concurring,
Its time I think, for me to think of stirring.

ABANAZAR. We'll make the pot boil here. Slave, mark the ground,
On which the shadow of yon tree is found,
Then, where the sand appears a little drier,
Gather some sticks and with them make a fire.

(KAZRAC does as directed--he measures forth the ground to the extremity of the shadow--then gather some stray sticks of which he makes a small heap, and rubbing two pieces of wood together at last kindles a spark and blows it with his breath into a flame. During this, ALADDIN shows his apprehensions increase, and ABANAZAR draws some small packets from his vest, showing also a small dagger.)

ALADDIN. Now if I can but quietly sneak off.
(As ALADDIN is creeping away, ABANAZAR coughs significantly.)
I'm going to get you something for your cough
Dear Uncle. There's a famous show I know
Where they sell lozenges that—let me go,
Its close to where we live—it's not remote—I'm
Safe to be there and back again in no time.

ABANAZAR. *(Threateningly producing dagger.)* Stay!

ALADDIN. Just one lozenge!

ABANAZAR. Stay!

ALADDIN. There's not taste in it,
  How cross you speak, I shan't be half a minute.

ABANAZAR. You stir not hence, you must be here a stopper.

ALADDIN. I won't!

ABANAZAR. You will!

ALADDIN. I shan't!

ABAMAZAR. *(Striking him.)* What's that?

ALADDIN. *(Rubbing his shoulder.)* A whopper.
  For twenty such, Aladdin doesn't care
  I don't believe you *are* my uncle! There!

ABANAZAR. *(Aside.)* I must dissemble! Better than before. *(Aloud.)* I like your spirit. There's my hand once more.

ALADDIN. Not in the same place unclie I'd advice you.

   *(He offers to defend himself, and then accepts the grasp of
     hand.)*

ABANAZAR. I want to show you something to surprise you.

ALADDIN. You did just now.

ABANAZAR. A cavern. One you see
  Of which you may the first discoverer be.

   *(ABANAZAR puts a packet of the charmed powder into the sire,
     a colored flame rises, stage grows dark, second powder thrown in.
     KAZRAC exhibits great terror as ABANAZAR compels him to
     assist in performing certain conjurations.)*

ABANAZAR. *(To ALADDIN.)* Now on your finger place this magic ring,
  Whilst in the flame the greatest charm I fling.

   *(As the Magician drops the powder into the flame, gong sounds,
     the root of the cedar crashes in two, and the stone with a brass
     ring appears.)*

ABANAZAR. *(Very loud.)* Here! raise this stone.

ALADDIN. *(To KAZRAC.)* Come, don't you hear you muff
  My uncle raises his tone high enough.

ABANAZAR. *(To ALADDIN.)* Your hand alone can bring to view the treasure.

ALADDIN. I don't believe it, but I'll try with pleasure.

(ALADDIN takes the brass ring in his hand, gong and the stone is raised to his great surprise, discovering a cavern.)

ALADDIN. There's a great cavern, and what's strange to me,
A lamp alight I underground can see.

ABANAZAR. *(In triumph.)* Tis mine! Aba! the lamp looks rather dimmer
Just hand it up to me, I'll get it trimmed.

ALADDIN. *(Descending.)* May I have all the pretty things I find?

ABANAZAR. All! only first give me the lamp to mind.
(Pushing ALADDIN down.)
We'll follow, just a little step, or two
I triumph! Ha! Ha! Cock-a-doodle do!

(ABANAZAR makes KAZRAC precede him and they disappear at the mouth of the cavern. Scene changes discovering—)

SCENE IV

The Garden of Jewels.

Rocky staircase, which ALADDIN is seen slowly descending as scene opens, avenue of tree bearing the jewel fruit. The Wonderful Lamp burning in recess. ALADDIN reaches centre and gazes admiringly around him.

ALADDIN. So far in safely I have found my way
Underground journeys seem the things to pay.
What curious tress and what strange fruits I can see,
There's been a good plum season here I have.
I'll try what one is like.
(Tries one.)
As hard as stone. Hard!
It can scarce be harder where there's none.
I'll pocket some for mother, though not juice full,
They may be on-a-mantel if not useful.

(Pockets fruit. ABANAZAR and KAZRAC appear at the opening above.)

ABANAZAR. The Lamp!

ALADDIN. I'm going uncle. How you are flurrying me.

ABANAZAR. The Lamp!

ALADDIN. I see it, what's the use of hurrying me.

ABANAZAR. *(Louder.)* The Lamp I say!

ALADDIN. *(Who has taken it.)* Permit me the remark—

ABANAZAR. Oh, drop it.

ALADDIN. *(Drops lamp.)* Done
    (Stage dark.)
There! now we're in the dark.

ABANAZAR. Fool! I meant drop the speech not let the light out.

ALADDIN. You should have said so then, I've put it quite out.

ABANAZAR. Quick! up the steps and give it to me, I say.

ALADDIN. I'd give it you if I could see my way,
    But as I can't you'll have to come to me.
    Much easier coming down than up must be.

ABANAZAR. Baffled, bamboozled! Be this cave your tomb,
    Dare to remonstrate, slave! Then share his doom.

> *(ABANAZAR hurls KAZRAC down into cavern, which closes
> with a loud noise as the stone rolls back over the aperture. Trial
> of KAZRAC how much his limbs have been injured by the fall
> and satisfactory result of the examination.)*

ALADDIN. Poor fellow. Tell me, are you hurt my man?
    Though with no tongue I don't see how he can,
    He tries to re-assure me. Well, I've heard
    Trust a man's actions rather than his word.
    *(KAZRAC expresses his horror of the Magician, his fidelity to
    ALADDIN and draws attention to ring.)*
    What's this! He thinks I've got a pretty ring.
    (Rubbing his hands.) Upon my word! This is a funny thing.

> *(Music. GENIE OF THE RING appears.)*

GENIE. Your wish! who holds that ring I quick attend up,
    What errand now your servant would you attend upon?

ALADDIN. My servant! you shall have if that's the case,
    The best of characters for your next place.
    I only want being disinclined to roam again,
    The ways and means of getting safely home again.

GENIE. For means these gems shall light you with their luster,
    Your homeward way lies through that diamond cluster.

(GENIE waves. Stage light and all the Fairies of the Jewels appear. Diamond conspicuous in centre Tableau.)

ALADDIN. Challenge the world they might for their attraction,
These are the jewels to give satisfaction.
Diamond, Pearl, Sapphire, Ruby, Garnet small,
Amethyst, Emerald, Topaz, welcome all.

DIAMOND. Behold as every gem around you whirls,
The graceful beauty of a string of pearls.
And brighter yet these jewels will be getting,
With skillful cutting, polishing, and setting.
Song of the Diamond
Deep in the mine, hid from the day,
Vainly we shine, wasted our ray,
Waiting the mortal, who values our worth,
Bidding us rank with the bright things of earth.
Thrilling the joy when the treasure displayed,
Tells of the toil by a pleasure repaid.
Dark in the mind, treasures will lie,
Waiting to find the warm beams of the eye,
Words that will lighten the heart till they seem,
Diamonds that brighten with sympathy's gleam.
Gems such as these did ye win from the shade,
Earth would a garden of jewels be made.

GRAND BALLET OF JEWELS

(Scene closing with tableau of Ballet, and KAZRAC and ALADDIN being conducted from cavern.)

SCENE V

Interior of Widow Ching's dwelling.

Enter WIDOW with draper's parcels under her arm. She arranges table, chairs, etc.

WIDOW. His uncle's face I think there's something bad in.
I wonder what he's done with Aladdin?
I don't half like our newly found relation,
Although he was improved our situation.
I've been out shopping—word which much expresses—
And bought the loveliest things in muslin dresses.
My money is all gone, it never lingers
'Midst linen-draper's shops in ladies fingers.

But uncle will, although he looks so grim
Take care of us.

(Enter ALADDIN and KAZRAC.)

ALADDIN. You had best take care of him.

WIDOW. Aladdin! (Embracing him.)

ALADDIN. Mother, safe I stand before you,
But that's no thanks to uncle I assure you.
Something's that's eatable pray quickly get,
Then hear with what adventures I have met.
My pockets full of fruit but they're detestable,
Nice to the eye but highly indigestible.
Here is a lamp, I don't know who will but it,
But it may sell for something. Take it—try it.

WIDOW. I never had, and ne'er had any other,
A lamp that didn't cause a deal of bother,
Either they won't burn, or they make a rum flare;
There's always something wrong about them somewhere.
I'll give it just a rub before I go,
Brighten! and back there's three and sixpence, oh!

(WIDOW rubs lamps. Thunder. GENIE OF LAMP appears.
KAZRAC and WIDOW falls on their faces.)

ALADDIN. And who are you?

GENIE. The Genie of the Lamp!
Whate'er you want I'll instantly decamp
And get.

ALADDIN. A dinner then for three, no less, sir.

GENIE. Dinner directly, dinner for three sir? yes sir!

(Banquet appears on table.)

ALADDIN. Magnificent!

WIDOW. (Recovering.) All laid out smart and tidily.
My boy has got a genie most decidedly.
(GENIE disappears.)
Delicious soup! I wonder what it's make of,
These foreign dishes one feels half afraid of.

(Whilst WIDOW eagerly partakes of everything, KAZRAC
clumsily assist.)

ALADDIN. Now mother, when your appetite's appeased.

WIDOW. With less of seasoning, better I'd been pleased.

ALADDIN. I say, when you appear, ma'am less voracious,
   Go to the Gham and ask him—

WIDOW. Cham! Good gracious!

ALADDIN. To take me for his son-in-law and say—

WIDOW. Oh, don't young man, you take my breath away.

ALADDIN. If he my princely offer thinks of scorning,
   His throne's not worth a sixpence in the morning.

WIDOW. The tailor's son, and wed a real Princess,
   I really couldn't ask it in this dress.

ALADDIN. Aye, there's the rub!
   (Rubs lamp. GENIE appears.)
   You have dresses made to measure!
   Three of the handsomest you have got.

GENIE. With pleasure.

   (The three appear magnificently attired.)

WIDOW. Well, really it's becoming I'll allow,
   If widow Grundy could but see me now!

ALADDIN. These costly presents he will not refuse;
   So rich a son-in-law he can't but choose.

   *(Music. ALADDIN loads the silver tureen with the jewel fruit,
   and WIDOW prepares to start. Tarter march heard. KAZRAC
   intimates the Royal Procession will soon pass the door, and
   expresses the dignity of the Cham, the beauty of Princess, and
   mechanical movements of the soldiers.)*

ALADDIN. You mean the Royal Procession is at hand.
   How well his signs I have learned to understand.

   (WIDOW'S courage fails her, her distrust.)

   Nay mother, of my suit he'll be no scorner,
   Quick, meet the monarch as he turns the corner.

   (ALADDIN hurries WIDOW off.)

   My fluttering heart with wild emotion stirs,
   Kazrac, look forth and tell me what occurs.

   *(KAZRAC places himself in position to command the view of
   the procession. ALADDIN interprets KAZRAC'S actions.)*

He sees her! Ha! the jewels he's aware of!
He hands them to a big man to take care of,
He nods his head! that nod there's something in,
And chucks mama on the maternal chin.
Points to this place! What's this, comes hither fast?
Then all my hopes are realised at last!

> (Enter in full procession the GRAND CHAM, Emperor of
> China, Tartar Dynasty, leading on the WIDOW, who is fully
> conscious of the great honour conferred upon her. The
> PRINCESS BADROULBADOUR and her attendants, headed
> by Zobeide, the Grand Vizier, Mandarins, Officers of State and
> the Tartar Guard.)

GRAND CHAM. Where is this most illustrious young man,
Who seeks alliance with great Cham-Chow-Khan?

ALADDIN. He stands your lofty mightiness before you.

GRAND CHAM. I'm very proud to meet you I assure you,
A Prince?

ALADDIN. Not quite. A traveller, whose opinions
Are highly fabourable to your dominions.
My wealth's unbounded, and my love's no less
For dear Badroulbadour, our fair Princess.

> (ALADDIN and PRINCESS talk apart.)

GRAND CHAM. Hum! very rich. He seems to be a catch.
What say we? Eh, Vizier? Is it a match?
> (GRAND CHAM and VIZIER whisper.)
A wise suggestion. Ere we have quite decided,
We would inquire what Palace is provided,
Befitting our illustrious daughter's station?

ALADDIN. Give me two minutes, choose the situation.
And I will have it built at once.

GRAND CHAM. Let's see!
The open space behind there.

ALADDIN. It shall be
> (Taking lamp aside.)
Quick Genie of the Lamp, a Place, one
Finer than ere was built.

GENIE. Conclude it done.

SCENE VI

Exterior of Aladdin's Palace.

GRAND CHAM. Can I believe these eyes now introduced to it?

ALADDIN. Oh, bless you, this is nothing when you are used to it!

GRAND CHAM. I'm perfectly bewildered.

PRINCESS. I'm delighted.

ALADDIN. To see the grounds, great Cham, you are invited,
My faithful servant will become your guide,
Whilst I some slight refreshment will provide.

> *(KAZRAC leads off the GRAND CHAM and the Court with great ceremony. the PRINCESS and ALADDIN remaining behind with ZOBEIDE and female attendants. AALADDIN sees lamp secure in vest.)*

PRINCESS. What wealth, what goodness, and what generosity—
What's that?

ALADDIN. A lamp dear, a mere curiosity,
A family relic, nothing I assure you.

PRINCESS. You said you loved me. *(Takes lamp.)*

ALADDIN. Love you! I adore you.

PRINCESS. And yet so near your heart this lamp to wear,
Suggests a flame in some old love affair.

> *(MANDERIN rushes in with VIZIER.)*

VIZIER. The Grand Cham wants one word explanatory.

ALADDIN. One moment, I'll return and tell the story.

> *(Exeunt ALADIN and VIZIER.)*

PRINCESS. Well, this is like a Palace I must say.
So large, we'll find new rooms out every day,
Though quickly built, there's nothing seems amiss.

> *(ABANAZAR the Magician heard without.)*

ABANAZAR. New lamps for old one.

PRINCESS. What strange man is this?

> *(Enter ABANAZAR as peddler with a tray of bright new lamps swung before him.)*

ABANAZAR. Who'll change old lamps for new?

(*Aside.*) From all I've heard I'm near my object.
(*Aloud*) Any old lamps?

PRINCESS. Absurd!

ABANAZAR. What change new lamps for old?
Yes Ma'am I'm playful.

PRINCESS. What would you give me now for this?

ABANAZAR. (*Eagerly.*) The tray full.

PRINCESS. I've half a mind, Aladdin then would see
He's found a treasure of a wife in me.
There! it's a bargain.

ABANAZAR. (*Throwing off disguise and seizing lamp.*)
Good! and there's the tray.
You've played the deuce! to Africa! away!

> (*Rapid music. Stage dark. ABANAZAR drags PRINCESS to Palace with ascends—borne by the Genie of the Lamp—and discovers—*)

SCENE VII

The place where it formerly stood.

A picturesque Chinese Landscape by moonlight, with winding river.

ALADDIN, KAZRAC, GRAND CHAM and entire Court, rush in amazed and despairing.

GRAND CHAM. Hi! Where's the Palace?

ALADDIN. No! Genie, keep close behind them.

> (*GENIE appears in Dragon, Chariot. KAZRAC and ALADDIN enter and go off in pursuit. The Chariot seen afterwards, in perspective, flying through the air. The whole of the Court, Guards, etc., appear with Chinese Lanterns, with which they keep up the excitement of an active search, and scene closes in on picturesque group, with stage completely illuminated by lanterns.*)

SCENE VIII

Interior of the Flying Palace, Africa.

Enter ABANAZAR the Magician, dragging in the Princess.

ABANAZAR. Who talks of infancy? that steam is in its—
A thousand leagues we've travelled in five minutes.
If you write home--my love and kind affection,
And say that "Africa," is our direction.
Should any peddler ask you, if you won't
Exchange old lamps--take my advice and don't.

PRINCESS. Unhand me, vile Magician quit my sight.

ABANAZAR. From such sweet lips that doesn't sound polite,
Especially when if I like to show it,
I could assume a hideous form.

PRINCESS. I know it.

ABANAZAR. Aha! sit down. Bestow one favoring smile,
I'll try the tender and impressive style.

(Music. ABANAZAR assumes the airs of a Court gallant, and expresses his love as a polished beau.)

Or p'raps you like a lover more romantic,
Behold him! jealous, furious and frantic.

(Imitation of another style of love-making in a more demonstrative fashion.)

Still not a word! Reflect that where I stand,
A hundred different forms I have at command,
Ogre, or polished Baron I supply,
Some here remember me a famous Guy.
No demon yet with which the world's acquainted,
Is half so black as W. H. Payne-ted.
One minute is allowed to each election,
Me for refreshment, you ma'am, for reflection.
My genius is the stupidest of fellers,
If with good wine he didn't stock the cellars.

(ABANAZAR sees all secure, then goes off.)

PRINCESS. Would that my loved Aladdin I could see.

(Enter ALADDIN and KAZRAC.)

ALADDIN. Behold!

PRINCESS. Can it be possible?

ALADDIN. It be!
Where's the Magician?

PRINCESS. Coming back I think.

ALADDIN. *(Gives small packet.)* This drug is poison, drop it in his drink.

He comes! the programme of this great Magician,
We thus enrich with one trick in addition.

> *(ALADDIN and KAZRAC conceal themselves behind couch, the latter gradually getting underneath the protruding his legs. Enter ABANAZAR slightly inebriated, with goblet and two large chopsticks.)*

ABANAZAR. Pardon Princess, if I have kept you waiting,
This wine is most exhil—exhil—arating,
So strong, I must see double I am sure.
I never noticed you had four legs before,
A rude young man, Princess, I may be thought to be,
But these are not so feminine as they ought to be.

> *(Drags forth KAZRAC by the legs whilst the PRINCESS drops the drug in goblet given her to hold.)*

Ha! ha! we'll have a little fun with some of you,
I wondered all this time what had become of you.

> *(KAZRAC defies ABANAZAR, who grows desperate, and a comic combat ensues with two large Pantomime Chinese chip-sticks. KAZRAC get ultimately the worst of it. The Magician refreshes himself from the poisoned goblet at the instigation of PRINCESS. He then see ALADDIN. Magician encounters both, the poison works, its peculiar effects on Magician, who finally subsides on couch. ALADDIN Secures lamp from his vest. GENIE appears.)*

ALADDIN. Behold the Lamp. The power remains the same.

GENIE. The lamp is yours. This wick-ness I claim.

> *(Seizing ABANAZAR. Couch flies off. Change to—*

Scene IX

The Efreets' Gloomy Haunt.

ALADDIN, PRINCESS, ABANAZAR, KAZRAC, ZOBEIDE and VIZIER at sides.

ABANAZAR. I'm a much better boy I beg to state.

GENIE. Well, if you are, repentance comes too late,
Justice to you a punishment accords.

(Enter the SPIRIT OF THE DIAMOND.)

DIAMOND. Whilst I am sent to give the good rewards
　　Aladdin and his Princess must perforce,
　　Live happy ever afterwards of course.
　　But whilst they are happy let us not believe,
　　In *this* world there is nothing left to Grieve.
　　The artist's eye see youthful fancy cling,
　　To Luna as the Genie of the Ring,
　　And shows how much more magical the ray
　　Of Earth's great gift, the wond'rous Lamp of Day

SCENE X

The Transformation Scene.

The Wondrous Lamp of Day!

DIAMOND. Kazrac the slave, still dumb may yet begin,
　　Existence happier as a Harlequin.
　　And fair Zobeide where his eyes incline,
　　Shall share his freedom as his Columbine.

　　(Changes KAZRAC to Harlequin. ZOBEIDE to Columbine.

GENIE. The roguish Vizier who vice here inherits,
　　As Pantaloon shall take the cuffs he merits.
　　Whilst Abanazar changed to pilfering Clown,
　　Shall show more tricks to mystify the town.

　　(Changes VIZIER to Pantaloon. ABANAZAR to Clown.

DIAMOND. Wit, whim, and wisdom, frolic, fancy fun,
　　Make our night's entertainment suit each one.

HARLEQUINADE

END

BEAUTY AND THE BEAST

Or

Harlequin and Old Mother Bunch

৵৹৶

(1869)

Beauty and the Beast was first performed at the Theatre Royal, Drury Lane, London, on December 27, 1869 with the following cast:

Ali, the Merchant....................... Brittain Wright

Scanderino, his Servant................ E. Fawdon Vokes

Zemira, "Beauty"......................... Victoria Vokes

Lamkinella, her sister.................. Harriet Coveney

Fatima, her sister......................... Rosina Vokes

Peri, a servant............................. Kate Santley

Chief Khorassan.......................... A. Rabb

Mirza, attendant on the Khan......... Master Summers

Zaid, female attendant................. Miss Hall

Zelma, Principal Peri................... Jessie Vokes

Spirit of the Rainbow.................. L. Grosvenor

Mother Bunch............................. Miss Hudspeth

Small Boy................................. Miss Lewis

Big Boy.................................... Master Russell

SCENE 1

Mother Bunch's "Juvenile Repository" for the sale of toys, sweetmeats, story-books, &c.

CHILDREN from "School" dispersed about the Stage, playing at hoop, kite, marbles, tops, riding-horse, hobby-horse, trap-bat and ball, cricket-bat, &c. As Curtain rises, a general "Hooray" from the BOYS, who are pointing at the LITTLE BOY.

SMALL BOY. Well, once upon a time, there lied a king
Who had three beauteous daughters---

BIG BOY. No such thing.

SMALL BOY. When one fine day a prince arrived at court,
So very handsome—

BIG BOY. Nothing of the sort.
I know the story. He had got a hunch.

SMALL BOY. No, this prince hadn't; just ask Mother Bunch.

OMNES. Ah! let's ask Mother Buuch. Hooray! hooray!

(Enter MOTHER BUNCH.)

MOTHER BUNCH. Why, hoity, toity! What's this hubbub, pray?
  I see, being out of "School," you think "Society"
  May cast aside, in play hours, all propriety.
  Half-holiday and Saturday afternoon!
  What, all my little ones! Tired of toys so soon.

BIG BOY. He's telling stories.

MORTHER BUNCH. Ah! then dread a whopper!

BIG BOY. I don't mean that. He doesn't tell them proper.
  You tell us one. We have read all those you sold.

MOTHER BUNCH. My tales, my dears, have, like myself, grown old.

OMNES. That's all the better.

MOTHER BUNCH. Well, you're not far wrong.
  Things must be good that last so very long.

Air—"When This Old Cap was New"

COME, ALL YOU LITTLE GENTLEMEN, AND LISTEN UNTO ME;
ALTHOUGH THE TIMES HAVE GREATLY CHANGED FROM WHAT
  THEY USED TO BE,
I DON'T THINK FASHIONS ALTER MUCH, OBSERVING LADIES, WHO
NOW DRESS EXACTLY IN THEIR GRANDMA'S USED TO DO.
AND SURELY THERE BE MANY HERE WHO KNOW THAT I SPEAK
  TRUE,
THE FASHIONS OF THE GOOD OLD TIMES WERE VERY LIKE THE
  NEW.

THE FAIRY TALES OF FORMER DAYS ARE STILL UPON THE TONGUE
OF ALL, WHEN ASKED TO TELL A PRETTY STORY TO THE YOUNG.
THE MODERNS CAN DO MANY TINGS, BUT CAN'T INVENT, I'M SURE,
A BETTER SORT OF FAIRY THAN THE ONE WE HAD BEFORE.
I WOULD NOT TAKE MY SOLEMN OATH THAT EVERY WORD WAS
  TRUE,
BUT THEN WE CAN'T BELIEVE, YOU KNOW, ALL STORIES THAT ARE
  NEW.

THE FOLKS WHO PRAISE THE PRESENT TIMES HAVE EARNESTLY
  DECLARED,

THE PEOPLE NE'ER WERE CHEAPER CLAD, AND NEVER BETTER
   FARED;
A SMALL AMOUNT OF MONEY NOW, I GRANT, WILL BUY A LOT,
BUT WHAT WE WANT TO KNOW IS—WHERE'S THE MONEY TO BE
   GOT?
AND SURE, I AM THAT MANY HERE WELL KNOW WHAT I SAY'S
   TRUE,
WE'VE READY HANDS TO DO THE WORK, WHO WANT THE WORK
   TO DO.

Good boys, like you, deserve to have a treat,
And Mother Bunch shall render yours complete.
Look round.
   (Flight of Ladybirds appear.)
A flight of ladybirds, that's all:
Such an assemblage isn't an uncommon 'up,
Though some have called it "Singular Phenomenon."
When you have seen these insects singly come,
You wisely bade them fly at once back home;
And giving youthful fancy free expansion,
Invented perils for their family mansion.
For kindly hints that took so wide a latitude,
They come to show their children—and their gratitude.

SMALL BOY. Perhaps some fairy in this form lies had.

MOTHER BUNCH. I shouldn't be astonished if it did.
Just for the jest—a little harmless merriment—
Suppose we venture on a small experiment.

   *(MOTHER BUNCH touches a LADYBIRD, and LITTLE
   LADYBIRD appears.)*

LADYBIRD. Dear Mother Bunch, I think you very much
For giving me that one improving touch.
You look as young as ever.

MOTHER BUNCH. Yes, my friend,
Age certainly improves my Grecian bend.
Blessed with eternal youths who think her clever,
Old Mother Bunch is "beautiful for-ever."
They want tale—don't mind how often heard—
A little id from Little Ladybird,
And I would give the best from my old store.

LADYBIRD. Most happy is assist you, ma'am, I'm sure.

MOTHER BUNCH. Then take your fight whilst I, on due reflection,

Decide what's best to choose from my collection.
"Bless you, my children!" I will not refuse you.

LADYBIRD. Come on, my little friends, and I'll amuse you.

(Exeunt LADYBIRD and CHILDREN.)

MOTHER BUNCH. Now to recall the Beast—revive the Beauty.
Ha! Good old Custom comes to pay his duty.
(OLD CUSTOM rises in Snap Dragon Car.)
Here with Snap Dragon I view prompt assistance.

OLD CUSTOM. My view don't lend enchantment to the distance.
I am an exile from my native land,
Banished for ever with my faithful band.
Folks say--but mean a different sense, no doubt—
A good old custom is the best thing—out.
Christmas is laughed at--chaps make fun of icicles,
The world's on wheels, and going mad on bicycles.
A levy of old customers see began,
Whose days were dwindled to the shortest span.
Twelfth Oake!

(Enter TWELTH OAKE.)

MOTHER BUNCH. Who once had characters to lose.

OLD CUSTOM. A Valentine!

(Enter a VALENTINE.)

MOTHER BUNCH. We now for albums choose.

OLD CUSTOM. Shrove Tuesday!

(Enter SHROVE TUESDAY.)

MOTHER BUNCH. Pancakes now last all the year.

OLD CUSTOM. The Oyster Grotto!

(Enter OYSTER GROTTO.)

MOTHER BUNCH. Doomed to disappear.

OLD CUSTOM. Guy Fawkes!

(Enter GUY FAWKES.)

MOTHER BUNCH. No longer what he was before.

OLD CUSTOM. And Dunmow Flitch!

(Enter DUNMOW FLITCH.)

MOTHER BUNCH. Which mus'n't be done more.

OLD CUSTOM. Here's half-a-dozen. All I have to spare of 'em;
And here I come to ask you to take care of 'em.

MOTHER BUNCH. Leave them with me. I'll see them well bestowed.
But hither come some others on the road,
An indication of more modern movements,
I must confess these seem to be improvements.
The Thames Embankment—well we can employ it.

(Enter EMBANKMENT.)

OLD CUSTOM. Let's hope the public will, ere long, enjoy it.

(Enter VIADUCT and BLACKFRIARS BRIDGE.)

MOTHER BUNCH. The Holborn Viabuct is warmly greeted,
With Blackfriars Bridge—colossal tasks completed.
Posterity may proudly point to those,
As best of all November's Lord Mayor's shows.
(Enter THMES TUNNEL.)
The Old Thams Tunnel made a Railway Station.
(Enter ELECTRIC TELEGRAPH.)
The Telegraph, now purchased by the nation.
(Enter SUEZ CANAL.)
And marvellous work--well kings might go and view it.
Such transformations, wrought by modern science,
May set all Mother's Bunch's t defiance.
Opening communications with the East,
At once we're off with "Beauty—

OLD CUSOM. And the Beast."

Air—"Wait for the Turn of the Tide"

MOTHER BUNCH.
BEWAILING IS WRONG; IN GOING THROUGH LIFE,
OPEN YOUR EYES BUT WIDE,
YOU'LL SEE, THOUGH HAVE RISEN THE WATERS OF STRIFE,
THERE'S ALWAYS AN EBB TO THE TIDE.
DON'T MAKE A BOTHER—YOU SHOULDN'T BY JEALOUS,
CUSTOMS FOLKS VALUE FAR MORE THAN THEY SEEM;
SAY, "WE WILL DO, MOTHER BUNCH, AS YOU TELL US,"
AND, DANCING AWAY, TAKE YOUR LEAVE OF THE THEME.

MOTHER BUNCH and **CHORUS.**
WE'LL MAKE YOU ALL HAPPY AND GAY, MY BOYS,
SO OPEN YOUR EYELIDS WIDE;
TO ROAM IN THE EAST WE'RE AWAY, MY BOYS,
AND WAIT FOR WHAT THERE WILL BETIDE.

(After Chorus, characters exeunt right and left. Change. The Evil Genii are seen exulting over the banishment of the Peri.)

SCENE II

The Vale of Cashmere

AZALKA, the expelled Peri, pleading for pardon, but is repulsed by ZELMA, the principal Peri.

ZELMA. Fixed the decree, and vainly you implore,
　　To happier regions you return no more,
　　Until atoned for is the great offence,
　　Which caused a Peri to be driven thence.

AZALEA. No more return? Is one of higher birth
　　Doomed then to be for ever on the earth?
　　I who have known the happiness to live.
　　Midst joys the duller world could never give;
　　A Peri of the realm, turned from these portals,
　　Obliged to share the common lot of mortals!
　　Well, I consider you have me been hard on.

ZELMA. But one thing only can secure your pardon,
　　You have been disobedient.

AZALEA. I admit it.

ZELMA. Not to say saucy.

AZALEA. That's the word, you have hit it.

ZELMA. For this you are expelled—a dreadful sentence!
　　Until not only have you shown repentance,
　　But can a sacrifice to goodness show,
　　Made by some maiden on the earth below.

AZALEA. Well, these are hard conditions you impose.
　　A sacrifice to goodness! Goodness knows
　　Where I shall ever find the one to make it.
　　But is these to appeal?

ZELMA. None!

AZALRA. None? Deuce take it!
　　I don't mean that--excuse the exclamation!
　　Forgive a Peir driven to desperation.
　　But really when one's under this correction,
　　One says the oddest things without refection.
　　Sisters, you see the fruits of being undutified.

I hope I am none the worse for being beautiful,
But that, I fear was how my fault arose.
Proud of my eyes, I upwards turned my nose.
Told what to do, I said at first—"I cant."
Again requested, rudely said—"I shan't."
Told for the third time with "Now, mind, beware!"
My pride was roused, and I replied, "Don't care!"
Thus came my dreadful punishment about.
Well, none of us know how we may turn out.

1ST PERI. My sympathy, dear sister, I bestow.

2ND PERI. And mine, regretting you are left below.

3RD PERI. All I can give is good advice. Pray don't
Let it occur again, you know.

AZALEZ. I won't.

3RD PERI. These things will happen, dear, among the best of us.
You thought yourself superior to the rest of us;
But Pride will have a fall.

1ST PERI. These things will happen, dear, among the best of us.
You thought yourself superior to the rest of us;
But Pride will have a fall.

2ND PERI. There is no controlling
Tempers like yours—

AZALEA. You both are most consoling.

2ND PERI. If you, for ever, dear, we leave behind.
We'll often think of you.

AZALEA. How very kind.
Upon my word I feel extremely grateful.
Such friends as these are positively hateful.
Is here no one kind sister of the air,
To bid me hope when driven to despair?

(The SPIRIT OF THE RAINBOW appears.)

RAINBOW. Borne on a cloud the banished one to cheer,
Behold the Spirit of the Rainbow near.
Song--Spirit of the Rainbow
Forth from the darkness of clouds in the sky,
Comes the bright Rainbow to gladden the eye;
Flinging around us its magical span
Bringing a token of gladness to Man.

Telling the world that the storm will depart,
Giving light to the Heavens and hope to the heart.
Shadows of sorrow by smiles chase away!
Trust in to-morrow when doubting to-day
Think of the sunlight and not of the gloom,
Sure that a rainbow the clouds will illume;
And remember the ray through the darkness appears
With the brightest of hues when it shines through our tears.

(Exit SPIRIT OF RAINBOW.)

AZALEA. My hopes revive. There comfort in that strain.
I'll wing my way to happier lands again;
And finding out true goodness on the earth,
Secure a treasure well a pardon worth.
Sisters, farewell. In humble garb I'll roam,
Till as a Peri you receive me home.
In mortal form I'll seek out virtue's track,
And with my prize triumphantly come back.

(Exit AZALEA.)

ZELMA. The fate of disobedience thus behold!
Let all beware not doing what they're told.
Now show the brightest honours which are shed
On those who mind exactly what is said.

GRAND BALLET
Ladies of the Corps de Ballet

SCENE III

The Caravanserai on the Borders of the Persian Desert.

GRAND ORIENTAL PROCESSION MARCH

*Arrival of the Caravan and Escort, and preparations for the journey.
Enter the Merchant ALI, accompanied by his three Daughters—
LANKINELLA, FATIMA, and ZEMIBA--the youngest known as
"Beauty"—attended by SCANDERINO, their Servant. Music.*

ALI. Quick! Coffee, sweetmeats, rice, and fruits for three,
And twice that quantity for one—that's me!
With much more room for stowage I'm endowed.
Here for refreshment half-an-hour's allowed;
So make the best of it. Though you remain,
I shan't soon get so good a chance again.

(ATTENDANT and a BOY bring on trays.)

BOY. Here be him coffee, massa; very nice!
    Him cake, him sweetmeat, melon, fig, and rice.

ATTENDANT. Pipes! pipes for travellers o'er the Desert going;
    The best tobacco of our native growing.

ZEMIRA. I have no appetite through thinking father,
    How soon you'll leave us.

LANKINELLA. Haven't I one? Rather!
    I'll take her share. I'm not at all dejected;
    But then that Beauty's always so affected.

FATIMA. I, too, can eat the whole of what they bring.
    Come, that belongs to me, you greedy thing.

ALI. Nay, nay, these little hands were never made
    To snatch each others victuals.

LANKINELLA. There, you jade!

ALI. You come to see your dad his road upon,
    And I, not you, should now be going on.
    Here is the station, daughters, where we part;
    For selling I must soon begin to start.

ZEMIBA. Father, I fear your losses were extensive.

ALI. My dear, your sisters have been both expensive,
    Whilst I confess that trade's been lately queer.
    And then the taxes for the following year
    Our Chancellor of the Exchanquer has decreed
    Must all be pain in this.

ZEMIRA. That's hard indeed!

ALI. In fact, of cash I'm getting very short;
    But I have a ship just reached a distant port,
    Which may bring profit, if the rogues will let it,
    And so your father goes himself to get it.

LANKINELLA. We'll have some precious fun whilst you are away.
    How long do you think you are likely, Pa, to stay?

ALI. It's a long journey. First, great rocks hang o'er us;
    Then sixty leagues the Desert spreads before us;
    Then, forty leagues beyond, we cross a plain;
    Then o'er a desert on we go again.
    Well, then we ought to leave behind the worst.

No—stop! we cross another desert first;
And then we ought—no, then, we cross a vale,
Where you see—bless me—thingumbobs for sale.
Then after that we come to--what's its name?
The famous town, called—Well, it's all the same.
And there, I hope, girls, to retrieve my losses.

LANKINELLA. The game you play, Pa,
Seems like "oughts" and "crosses."
Bother the journey—never mind the track
What are you going to bring us coming back?

ALI. Ah! girls, I see you think my duties to
Include Pa-rental and pay taxes too!

LANKINELLA. Oh, bring for me, Papa, a handsome dress,
The handsomest that money can procure.
You'll not refuse that money can procure.
You know, Papa, than Fatima I'm bigger.
And ought to sow I have got a graceful figure.

FATIMA. Lot of jewels, P, is my desire,
That girls may envy me, and men admire.

ALI. And now, my youngest, come, your wish explain.

ZEMIRA. Papa, I want—to see you back again;
To see you safe at home, all perils past,
As well as when you parted from us last.

LANKINELLA. What affectation! Don't believe a word!

ALI. Want nothing, Beauty?

ZEMIRA. Nothing!

LANKINELLA. How absurd!

ALI. I must bring something for you.

ZEMIRA. Then suppose you simply bring your daughter back a rose.
Receiving this, dear father, I shall say
You kindly thought of me when far away.

LANKINELLA. I boil with rage. A rose! To look about for it!
When we get home, oh! won't I serve her out of it.

SCANDERINO. The time is up. The caravan proceeds.

ALI. Pack up, then, all the luggage that one needs.

Air—"It's Nice to be a Father"

THE CAMEL BELLS ARE RINGING OUT, WE MUST BE OFF AT ONCE.
SCANDERINO MOVE ABOUT—HE IS THE BIGGEST DUNCE!
IF ANY ONE SHOULD ASK ME WHY HIM I DO EMPLOY.
I'M SURE I COULDN'T TELL THEM MORE THAN ANY BABY BOY.
IT'S NICE TO BE A FATHER OF THREE SUCH BEAUTIES--RATHER;
IT'S FINE TO BE A PARENT, BUT PRAY DON'T WISH ME JOY;
THOUGH I ALWAYS LET THEM KNOW THAT I'M THEIR PA!

LANKINELLA and **FATIMA**.
YES, WE ALWAYS LET HIM KNOW THAT HE'S OUR PA.

ALI. Come, Scanderino, pack up all to start,
And see the camels ready to depart.
Bismillah! what an oversight!

LANKINELLA. Good gracious!
Lost anything, Papa?

ALI. Well, how vexatious!

FATIMA. What is the matter?

ALI. Well, I never thought of it.
Really that is about the long and short of it.

ZEMIRA. Papa, what is it?

LANKINELLA. Yes, what is it? Say.

ALI. Our only servant I have brought away,
He's a good for little, but with virtues small,
He still was better than not one at all.
Among the crowd here p'r'aps I may discern
Some one to take his place till we return.
I want a servant. Who with me engages.

(Enter AZALEA, the Peri, disguised as SUSLANA the Servant.)

AZALEA. Happy to serve you, sir, for moderate wages.
The best of characters I with me bring.

(Presents scroll.)

ALI. Well, let me see. It seems about the thing.
These are my daughters; you will serve the three
When I am gone, on terms you can agree
We must be off. Come, Scanderino, bustler
And load the camels to their very muzzle.

*(Music. Preparations for the journey. ALI takes leave of his
Daughters, kissing ZEMIRA only--Jealousy aroused in the other*

Daughters. Arrival of the Camels—loading them.
SCANDERINO thoughtfulness, &c.)

Air—"Monkey's Courtship"

ALI.

LANKINELLA NOW MIND YOUR SISTER.
BEAUTY KNOWS THAT HER FATHER'S KISSED HER.
THANK YOU FOR A LEG UP, MISTER
COME, THAT'S PRETTY WELL!
THE CAMEL SEEMS TO KNOW ITS MASTER.
BLESS ME! THERE! I CAN'T STICK FASTER;
IT WOULD BE A BAD DISASTER
OFF HIM I FELL.

LANKINELLA.

GOOD-BYE DAD; I'LL MIND MY SISTER;
SHE SHALL KNOW HER FATHER KISSED HER.
I'LL STICK TO HER LIKE A BLISTER;
WON'T I MAKE HER YELL!

(Chorus repeated—OMNES.)

NEVER CARRIED SO GOOD A MASTER;
TAILS FOR CAMELS CAN'T RESIST
MILD PERMISSION LIKE A TWISTER.
OFF WE GO!—ALL'S WELL!

(The Caravan is formed, and goes off in grand procession. The
Three Sisters and AZALEA left watching the departure.)

LANKINELLA. Now the, you hypocrite, come, dry that tear,
Or you shall cry for something—never fear.

FATIMA. Because she thinks she's prettier than we are,
She gives herself all kinds of airs. Oh! de—ar!

AZALEA. Amongst these two it would be vain to seek.

LANKINELLA. Now I'm your mistress.—Come, how much a week?

AZALE. Small wages give, to serve you I'll be proud.

LANKINELLA. No Sundays out--no followers allowed;
Smart caps forbidden—hair worn short behind.
You will dress us and not yourself—pray mind.
No perquisites—month's notice—that's to say,
On your side. We dismiss you any day.
And this agreed upon the bargain striking,
I'll take you, without payment, upon liking.

AZALEA. Your offer, madam, I shall not decline.

ZEMIRA. Poor girl! her fate will be as hard as mine.

Solo—(Operatic)—Zemira

OH, SAD IS THE FATE I ENDURE
MY SISTERS THEIR YOUNGER ONE SPURN;
THEY VEX ME, BUT STILL I AM SURE
I BEAR NO ill will in return.

Air—with variations

LANKINELLA.

I HAVE THE LEAST IDEA, SO FAR,
OF WHO YOU ARE; BUT MY PAPA,
I KNOW, IS VERY PARTICULAR—
AND HE SEEMS TO SEE NO BAR.
AH! AH! AH! AH! AH! AH!
SO I REALLY THINK YOU'LL DO—DO—DO

AZALEA.

I WAS BORN AND BRED HERE IN THE EAST,
AND HOPE AT LEAST YOU WON'T HAVE CEASED.
TO KEEP ME TILL YOU HAVE INCREASED
MY WAGES MORE THAN THEY ARE.
AH! AH! AH! AH! AH! AH!
OR ELSE THEY WILL NOT DO—DO—DO

LANKINELLA, FATMIA, ZEMIRA

HOME WITH US—IT ISN'T FAR;
WE'LL HAVE CAR; IT WILL JOLT AND JAR,
BUT WE MUSTN'T BE TOO PARTICULAR,
SO DON'T MAKE ANY ADO.

AZALEA. *(Singing at the same time.)*

HOME WITH YOU, AS IT ISN'T FAR;
YOU'LL HAVE A CAR; IT WILL JOLT AND JAR,
BUT I MUSTN'T BE TOO PARTICULAR.
SO SHAN'T MAKE ANY ADO.

(Dance and exeunt.)

SCENE IV

Forest of Apes

Melodramatic Music and Action.

ALI and SCANDERINO, arrested in their journey by Arab Robbers, are brought in as prisoners, and being plundered, are rescued from further violence by the timely appearance of unexpected aid. The Robbers receive "Monkeys" allowance, and disappear.

ALI. Oh! Scanderino! Scanderino, oh!

SCANDERINO. O! master, master! here's a precious go.

ALI. There's nothing left in all the caravan;
    I have no more. You have taken all you can.
    Our guards have taken flight. Put up your knives;
    Take anything you like, but spare our lives.
    Don't, there's a good young man. Oh! what a dig!
    Respect grey hairs, if even in a wig.
    It's not your fault you chose this occupation;
    It's only your neglected education.
    I don't blame you, I only blame society.
    Killing is tedious work—it lacks variety.
    Suppose you don't stick us, but let us go;
    It would be quite a novelty, you know.
    My good friend, remember you had a mother—
    Oh! there's a poke--who nursed you--There's another.
    Perhaps a father, too. Oh! that's a teazer.
    Come, I say, none of that fun, if you please, sir.

    (ALI and SCANDERINO gain courage and "persuade" their kind friends to leave them. After some trouble they succeed.)

ALI. Whew! I am out of breath! Oh, here's a plight!
    A dreary forest and a stormy night!
    No earthyly power can from perils free us.
    What would my daughters think, could they but see us?
    Why did we both set out? I'm stupid grown,
    Or I should have let you journey forth alone,
    And proved to Scanderino, now disgusted,
    How well my faithful servant could be trusted.
    The very heavens our journey seem to frown upon.
    Oh! if we had only something to sit down upon.

    (Two chairs come on.)

What have we here? Two seats. Well, these being found
We shall not come, between them, to the ground.
A table now would quite complete my wishes,
Especially if spread with savoury dishes.

    (Table come on.)

Well, this is kind of somebody; however
To do this banquet justice, I'll endeavour.

(*SCANDERINO, frightened, persuades his mast not to partake of refreshment supplied in so mysterious a manner.*)

ALI. Don't be afraid—there's plenty of it, look!
Upon my word, he keeps a splendid cook.
Fruits are delicious, everything entrancing;
All that we want is music and some dancing.

(*Mysterious music.*)

SCENE V

Palace of Prince Azor

Grand Persian Ballet
By the Ladies of the Corps de Ballet
In which will introduced the celebrated "Bells" mazurka

ALI. Come, very good indeed. This grows exciting.
The banquet glorious; flowers most inviting.
Now then to pluck a rose, for Beauty's share.
This will be quite the thing for her.

AZOR. (*Without.*) Forbear!

ALI. So generous with your viands, who supposes
You are going to be so stingy with your roses?

AZOR. (*Without.*) Forbear, I say.

ALI. Oh! nonsense. Off I twist it;
It looked so tempting, I could not resist it.

(*Gong. Enter PRINCE AZOR as the Beast.*)

AZOR. Sol this is your return for all I have done.
You steal my roses.

ALI. Only taken one.

AZOR. That's quite enough. When travellers come to sup,
And rob their host, they must be taken up.

ALI. I have got no money, or would pay for it heartily.

AZOR. Ah! you will have to pay for it pretty smartly.
You have well been entertained at my expense.
And now my favorite rose you have stolen hence.
I've good mind to eat you.

ALI. To make free with you,
I'm sure on that point I should disagree with you.
But, most illustrious monster, let me say,
Not for myself took I that flower away
But for my daughter, who a rose desired—
Only a rose, and noting more required.

AZOR. Merchant of such respectable condition,
I am grieved to see you placed in this position.
But, prisoner at the bar, I'll justice render;
I look up you as an old offender.
You are brought before me charged with stealing those
Twelve leaves and stalk—to wit, one damask rose.
With certain odours which from them transpire,
The personal property of Dash Beast, Esquire.
The evidence is clear—you cannot shake it;
There is the rose—the owner say you take it.
The sentence is—

ALI. Oh, don't, sir! On my knees
I ask for pardon. Do forgive me, please.
Do let me off. It ne'er occurred before.
Only this time. I won't do it any more.
Think of my daughter—

AZOR. I must do my duty.
Your daughter's name?

ALI. Please sir, we call her Beauty.
So like her poor old father in the face.

AZOR. The daughter, then, shall take the father's place.

ALI. Huzza! You let us go?

AZOR. I set you free.
On this condition—Beauty comes to me.

ALI. Well, I must say, you do want Beauty badly.

AZOR. Is it a bargain?

ALI. One I make most gladly.
But Beauty minds my house. Would I were in it.

AZOR. I move my club. You are both home in a munute.

Song
Air—"I Was an Artful Dodger"

AZOR.

I'M NOT VERY HANDSOME, BUT YOU WELL MAY UNDERSTAND
I'M RICH ENOUGH TO MARRY ANY LADY IN THE LAND.
I HAVE A ROUGH OUTSIDE, BUT THEN MY FEELINGS ARE ACUTE,
AND SO REFINED, THEY CALL ME HERE THE LARDY-DARDY
 BRUTE.
GET READY FOR YOUR JOURNEY--YOU WILL QUICKLY HAE TO
 START;
AND TELL YOUR DAUGHTER BEAUTY SHE MUST INSTANTLY
 DEPART.
I WAIT FOR HER IMPATIENTLY, AND SHALL HAVE REST NO MORE,
UNTIL I GET THE BEAUTY WHICH I WANTED SO BEFORE.
THEN YOU MAY GO AND TELL HER I'M A MAN OF PROPERTY,
FUNDED, PERSONAL, AND HAVING MANY LAND;
AND IF SHE WANTS TO SEE WHAT A HUSBAND OUGHT TO BE,
SHE CAN FIX THIS JOLLY PARTY IN THE MATRIMONIAL BANDS.

*(Comic Shadow Dance. After which AZOR waves his club.
SCNDERINO vanishes.)*

SCENE VI

Interiors of Ali's House.

ALI discovered sleeping on a couch.

ALI. Where am I? Surely a well-known locality.
 It looks—it is—it must be a reality.
 Home once again, and safe! Delightful thought!
 I can't exactly say how I was brought,
 But here I am. The means I can't make out,
 But that I am here won't admit of doubt.
 How gladly will my daughters rush to greet me.

 *(Noise without. ALI retires up the back. Enter LANKINELLA,
 driving in ZEMIRA and slapping her.)*

LANKINELLA. Take that—and that!

ZEMIRA. Is that the way to treat me?
 I have done nothing to deserve this blow.

LANKINELLA. Why didn't you, then, I much should like to know?
 I'll teach you to do nothing! Nothing—stuff!
 You take the servant's part—that's quite enough.

 (Enter FATIMA, driving in AZALEA, still disguised.)

64

FATIMA. I'll give it you for singing at your work.
A pretty singer *you* are!

AZALEA. *(Aside.)* What a Turk!
Since I've been here, you two have much ill-used me,
Knocked me about, and shamefully abused me.
I have tried to please—worked hard from morn till night,
But nothing that I do seems ever right.

LANKINELLA. Of course it isn't! You are a precious lot.
I'll let you see the missus you have got.

ZEMIRA. I wish dear father could return to-day.

LANKINELLA. I dare say that you do. He's miles away.
So, then, you little tell-tale, you'd have told him;
But, know, he won't be back for months.

ALI. *(Advancing.)* Behold him!
I have heard all.

LANKINELLA. Oh, father, I'm delighted!
Now for the dress, and then you'll see me righted.

ALI. Something has happened—that you may suppose;
All I have with me brought is Beauty's rose.

ZEMIRA. Dear Pa! what's happened? Oh, how kind to bring it.

ALI. It's a long tale to tell; I'd better sing it.

Air—"Strolling in the Burlington"

THE CARAVAN GOES SOMETIME ON, AS PLEASANT AS CAN BE,
THOUGH RIDING ON A CAMEL'S BACK WITH MINE DOES NOT
    AGREE.
THE MERCHANTS HAVE A CHAT, AND THE SOLDIERS THEY PARADE,
AND ERE THE SUN HAS SET, GREAT PROGRESS WE HAVE MADE.
AND NOBODY SEEMED IN THE LEAST AFRAID;
JOLTING WENT THE CAMELS ON, SPLENDIDLY ARRAYED;
STROLLING ON, WHAT FUNNIMENTS WE PLAYED.
I WOULD YET GO FURTHER ON, AND FURTHER ON I STRAYED.

Change of Air—"When a Man Weds"

SUDDENLY OUT—ARABS ABOUT—
SPY AWAY, FLY AWAY, FIX FIX;
TUMBLE US DOWN—TAKE EVERY CROWN;
ROBBERY, ROBBERY, QUICK STICKS;
MERCHANT ESCAPES, FOREST OF APES,
LAUGHERY, CHAFFERY, GRIN, GRIN;

SNIP OFF A ROSE—THEN THE GREAT NOSE
OF A TERRIBLE MONSTER POPS IN;
WON'T LET US GO, SAYS HE MUST KNOW
THE GIRL IT IS FOR, AND WHY IS IT;
TELL HIM HER NAME, AND PRESTO! I CAME
TO SAY YOU MUST PAY HIM A VISIT.
ROBBERY, ROBBERY, LAUGHERY, CHAFFERY, ROSARY, POSERY;
HURRYING, SCURRYING, CRASH ALONG, DASH ALONG.

(Spoken.) If you would learn the events of the road,
    This is the channel in which they have flowed.
    You wanted to know where your father had been,
    Well these are his ventures—adventures he really has seen.

LANKINELLA. What, not a dress? Of course my passion flies out.

FATIMA. And I no jewels! I could cry my eyes out.

ZEMIRA. I have the rose, and better still, my father.

AZALEA. I fancy there's a chance for me here—rather.
    I think mum, you forget, mum please, that master
    Told you that rose brought on him some disaster.
    Where be obtained that flower you have to do.

ALI. My child, what Susiana says *is* so.
    I promised you should see the place, at least;
    But then the owner of it is a beast!

ZEMIRA. If you have promised, Father, that's enough.
    I'm not afraid of him. I feel audacious.
    If this was him—

AZOR. *(Without.)* Forbear, I say!

ALI. Good gracious!
    He's everywhere at once.

ZEMIRA. I'll take our maid;
    She shall attend me. I am not afraid,
    So off I go. You plucked the rose for me,
    And gave a promise which redeemed shall be.
    All that I want, Pa, is the right direction.

LANKINELLA. And this she calls a sisterly affection!
    I have not patience with her leaving us.

FATIMA. And making, of a paltry rose such stuff.

ALI. Ah, child! If Scanderino now was near!
    But I'm afraid he'll never more appear.

The Beast just waved his club--the man bewitchin'—

(Enter SCANDERINO, with toasting fork and cake.)

SCANDERINO. Oh! here's a lark! I've turned up in the kitchen.
What a nice fellow-servant I have go.
This has a little moved you.

AZALFA. Not a jot.

Air—"The Bell It Keeps Ringing for Sarah"

ALTHOUGH I AM BUT A DOMESTIC,
OR WHAT YOU WOULD CALL "SERVANT GAL,"
I WILL NOT BE WORRIED AND FLURRIED,
THOUGH SOME MAY INSIST THAT I SHALL.
I'M READY TO GO WITH YOUNG MISSIS,
TO SEE HOW THIS BRUTE MAY APPEAR
A PROMISE, WHEN MADE JUST AS THIS IS,
SHOULD ALWAYS BE KEPT, IT IS CLEAR.
FOR NOTHING, I THINK, CAN BE FAIRER, FAIRER, FARIER,
NOTHING, I THINK CAN BE FAIRER,
THAN DOING THE THING WHICH IS RIGHT.

Air—"Cackle, Cackle"

YOU SAUCY SUSIANA, I SHALL GIVE YOU WARNING.
ON ME YOU SHOULD HAVE WAITED WHEN MISS BEAUTY WAS
    ADORNING.
YOUR CONDUCT REALLY CAUSES ME A DEAL OF AGITATION,
AND NOW I GIVE YOU WARNING YOU MUST LEAVE YOUR
    SITUATION.
OH! CHATTER, CHATTER, CHATTER! YAWNING ALL THE MORNING.
NOTHING YOU WILL DO AT ALL. I SHALL GIVE YOU WARNING,
WAITING ON BEAUTY WHEN I WANT ADORNING.
COOK, COOK, COOK, COOK, COOK, COOK, WHAT YOU OUGHT TO
    DO.

(Chorus repeated to business, and OMNES exeunt, dancing.)

SCENE VII

The Palm-Tree Grove.

Enter SCANDERINO, leading on ZEMIRA and AZALEA, from left.

AZALEA. We want no guide; so, Scanderino hence with you.
You have served us well, but here we can dispense with you.
My missus and myself can find the way—

You needn't fear that we shall go astray.

ZEMIRA. The Beast resides not far from here, I'm sure;
I almost fancy I can hear him roar.

SCANDERINO. Oh! Susiana, if you only knew.

AZALEA. Don't, Mr. S., you'll be a mischief-maker.
I have had a splendid offer from the baker.
Besides, young man, remember, if you please,
This don't improve your small clothes at the knees.

SCANDERINO. You'll let me talk to you, Susy, whilst you are cooking?

AZALEA. Oh, go along now, do; there's missus looking!

(Exit SCANDERINO, kissing her hand.)

ZEMIRA. Now that my plan is put in execution,
I fear I waver in my resolution;
My foolish heart is trembling whilst pursuing it.

AZALEA. It's for your father, miss, you know you are doing it.

ZEMIRA. I hope the Beast is not so very frightful!

AZALEA. Master describes his gardens as delightful.

ZEMIRA. But, then, his ugly face and awful figure!
I shouldn't mind if I was only bigger;
But, being so little, don't you think it's wrong?
It looks so bold of me, when he's so strong.

AZALEA. Your father made a promise.

ZEMIRA. So he did.

AZALEA. You wouldn't have him break it?

ZEMIRA. Truth forbid!
I was but thinking what he now would say,
If he could see me going on this way.

AZALEA. *(Aside.)* I find I must not magic art pursue.
Hear what your father thinks you ought to do.

(AZALEA waves her hand. The Palm Trees open and disclose, as in a vision, the form of ALI, the Merchant.)

Air—"Act on the Square"

MY BEAUTY, GO ON ACTING RIGHT, STRAIGHT FORWARD WALK,
AND THERE

A PALACE SOON WILL MEET YOUR SIGHT, AND LITTLE NEED YOU
   CARE.
AS HAPPY AS A KING YOU MAKE YOUR FATHER, WHOM YOU SPARE;
SO, FROM EXPERIENCE I GIVE THIS HINT--ACT ON THE SQUARE.
ACT OF THE SQUARE GIRL, ACT ON THE SQUARE;
UPRIGHT AND FAIR, GIRL, ACT ON THE SQUARE.
ALWAYS, MY DEAR GIRLS, DO WHAT IS FAIR;
TELL EVERY CIRCLE TO ACT ON THE SQUARE.

   (Branches close. ALI disappears.)

AZALEA. Better advice, I'm sure, could not be heard.
   Yes, yes, dear father, you shall keep your word;
   I make this sacrifice, for your sake, gladly.

   (Exit ZEMIRA.)

AZALEA. Well, come, I think I haven't managed badly.
   Here *is* a sacrifice; nor made in vain,
   If, through it, I a Peri's place regain.

   (Exit AZALEA. Enter LANKINELLA and FATIMA.)

LANKINELLA. This way she came. I wonder how he'll treat her?
   Whether the Beast will marry her, or eat her?
   If he has any taste, I think he'll see,
   Waning a wife, he should have chosen me.
   He's rich, of course, so, if a wife he took,
   I think his figure we might overlook.

FATIMA. That's my opinion, Lankinella, dear;
   But *I* should much more suitable appear.

   (Exeunt.)

SCENE VIII

The Wilderness.

*Enter the BEAST and his transformed Attendants much dejected;
followed by two DOCTORS, with bottles labelled "Laughing Gas" and
"Cordial."*

AZOR. Plenty of time I gave him home to get,
   But Beauty, promised, hasn't turned up yet.
   She comes not; deary me, and lack-a-day,
   Each lingering minute sees me pine away.
   Vainly you try my drooping hopes to cheer.
   Attendants, vanish! Doctors, dissapear!

With nothing in the universe I'm pleased.
Say, can'st thou minister to a mind deseased,
Pluck from the memory a rooted sorrow,
Or wisely say to me, "How do you do to-morrow?"
Of course you can't. A bottle! make some fun of it;
Throw physic to the dogs, for I'll have none of it.

(AZOR scatters the Attendants, who exeunt.)

I feel each joint is getting loose the looser.
I ask for Beauty! Was, but what's the use, sir?

(AZOR indulges in a collapsing dance.)

Air—"Original"

ALL'S DONE! HERE'S ONE, DEPRIVED OF HIS DESIRES;
QUITE YOUNG, FEELS HUNG, MORE AND MORE, ON WIRES.
ONE—TWO—THREE-FOUR—BIT BY BIT HE GOES,
LIKE THE THINGS WE USED TO SEE IN FANTOCCINI SHOWS.

ARMS OUT, NO DOUBT--BOTH ARE MUCH PERPLEXED;
LEGS QUEER—NO IDEA—WHERE THEY'LL GO TO NEXT;
RIGHT, LEFT—LEFT, RIGHT—ALL SEEMS COMING OFF;
SHOULDN'T WONDER IF I FOUND MY SKIN I OUGHT TO DOFF.

(Collapses at Fountain. Enter ZEMIRA.)

ZEMIRA. I hope for my appointment I'm not late.
I'm quite prepared, so let me know my fate.
All silent! Say, oh! tell me whom I seek, oh!
Say, can addition—

ECHO. Second edition-E-cho.

ZEMIRA. What mockery is this? I should escape any—
This garden seems so lonely.

ECHO. Only a ha'penny!

ZEMIRA. I tremble at these sounds. Ah! what do I see?
It seems—it is—that face—that form—'tis he!
Poor Beast! Oh, why was I not here before?
This disappointment killed him, I am sure.
Oh, why not stay till Beauty did arrive;
I would have loved you, had you been alive.

AZOR. *(Revives.)* You really mean it? Then say what you can of me;
No more a Beast--your love that made a man of me.

(Resumes his shape as a Prince.)

ZEMIRA. A Prince!

AZOR. Prince Azor! doomed here thus to dwell,
Till woman's love could break the magic spell.

(Enter FATIMA.)

FATIMA. Not eaten up! I'm first to reach the station.

AZOR. Your sister? Come, a dance of exultation!

Dance—AZOR and BEAUTY
(Dance of exultation.)

YES, THAT ROSE FROM YONDER BOWER
GIVE TO ME/HIM THIS HAPPINESS NOW,
AND FRESH JOYS WITH EVERY HOUR;
GIVE TO LOVE—TO LOVE—SWEET REPOSE.
SO WE LOVE—WE LOVE THIS FAIR ROSE.
MERRILY SO, MERRILY NO;
DANCING ABOUT, NEVER TIRED OUT;
IF WE ENDEAVOUR—DANCING FOR EVER.
WE UP AND WE UP, AND WE UPWARD GOES.

(Enter LANKINELLA, improved in personal appearance.)

LANKINELLA. All my bad temper's gone, through your advice.

ZEMIRA. Ah! that's the reason that you look so nice!

(Enter AZALEA as Peri.)

AZALEA. This sacrifice fulfilled--I've kept my vow;
My task performed, receive me, sisters, now.
(Waves her wand, and Grand Transformation to—)

The Fortunate Islands

ZELMA. Azalea, you have well your pardon earned;
A cordial greeting welcomes you returned.
To give to mortals pleasures they can share,
A pantomimic party I'll prepare.
Old Custom's voice is heard in Drury Lane.
Exclaiming, "Hallo! here we are again!"

Harlequinade

END

JACK IN THE BOX

Or

Harlequin Little Tom Tucker,

and

The Three Wise Men of Gotham

৯৶৶

1873

Jack in the Box opened at the Drury Lane, London December 26, 1873 with the following cast:

Ralph Roysterdoyster	Mr. Hogan
Richard Higgledypiddledy	Mr. Naylor
Robin de Robbin	Mr. Lickford
Prince Felix	Miss Harriet Coveney
Jack in the Box	Mr. F. Evans
Cockalorum the Great	Mr. Brittain Wright
Princess Poppet	Miss Alma Murray
Grand Chamberlain	Mr. Bigwid
Court Physician	Mr. Goldnob
Lord High Treasurer	Mr. Pursy
Chief Justice	Mr. Wisywersey
Chancellor of Exchequer	Mr. Chinks
President of Council	Mr. Winks
Master of the Horse	Mr. Blinks
Queen Elfina	Miss Sylvia Hodson
Harmonia	Miss Russell
Fairy Cornucopia	Miss Mowbray
Little Tom Tucker	Miss Amalia
Little Bo-Peep	Miss Violet Cameron

SCENE I

View of the Village of Gotham Sunset with Saw Mill, Brook, and Timber Yard.

Music. The THREE WISE MEN and all the VILLAGERS of Gotham discovered busily looking for needles in bundles of hay, as curtain rises to symphony of opening chorus.

Air—Old English "The Maypole"

CHORUS.
> WE'VE SEARCHED ABOUT, BUT CAN'T FIND OUT
> THE PLACE WHERE THEY CAN BE;
> THO' IN AND OUT, AND ROUND ABOUT
> THAT PLACE WE'VE TRIED TO SEE.
> THEY SHOULD BE SOMEWHERE HERE,
> AND OUGHT TO BE, WE SAY;
> BUT WE'VE STUMBLED, GRUMBLED, MUMBLED, FUMBLED,
> TUMBLED ABOUT THE HAY.
> TUMBLED, FUMBLED, MUMBLED, GRUMBLED,
> STUMBLED ABOUT THE HAY.

RALPH. Well, have you got 'em?

RICHARD. Got 'em? we can't find 'em.
> These bundles must have left them all behind them.

ROBIN. Looking for needles here we've been all day.

RALPH. Yet that's the place to look for them, folks say.

ROBIN. Well, possibly a bowl requires no stitching.

RICHARD. Sagacious thought! that notion is bewitching.
> Better the planks should pasted be together,
> Then they will bid defiance to the weather.

RALPH. We have been called, by men of every nation,
> The greatest set of boobies in creation;
> But after this, a question will arise
> Whether the men of Gotham are not wise.

ROBIN. A few tin tacks would not be a bad plan;
> We'll nail the planks together, if we can.

RALPH. Tin tacks! the very thing, I have no doubt.
> Haven't you heard that ships take tacks about?

RICHARD. At all events, we three are on the whole

All bent on going to sea,

RALPH and **ROBIN**. And in a bowl.

RALPH. Then for provision, stores we must lay in
  (Note of Cuckoo.)
  Hark! there's a cuckoo! Let us hedge him in.

  *(Music. As the Cuckoo hops on with his familiar note, ROBIN,
  RALPH, and RICHARD, with the rest of the Men of Gotham,
  hide each behind a Bundle of Hay gradually hopping down, they
  enclose the Cuckoo, leaving him however visible to audience.)*

RALPH. This is a clever notion, I must say
  We have him safe.

  (Cuckoo goes over their heads and exits.)

OMNES. Look! See! He flies away!

  *(Quick music. Fruitless chase of VILLAGERS, who fling off
  their bundles of hay after Cuckoo. ROBIN brings on three
  cheeses.)*

ROBIN. Here are three cheeses.

RICHARD. Cheeses? We want meat.

RALPH. Of course, we beef and mutton ought to eat.
  Send them to market, they will sell themselves;
  And what they bring we'll place upon our shelves.

RICHARD. There, roll them down the hill. They know the way,

RALPH. And fetch good prices, for it's market day.

  (The three Cheeses are rolled off.)

ROBIN. I wish I'd sheep as there are stars on high.

RICHARD. And I a field as big as the whole sky.
  You shouldn't graze your sheep, tho', in my field.

ROBIN. Oh ! wouldn't I.

RICHARD. No that point I'd never yield.

ROBIN. Then, let this teach thee that I would and will.

RALPH. Forbear! A stranger's coming up the hill,
  Of noble presence, tho' in humble guise,
  He may assist us he looks very wise.

(Music. Enter with bundle over his shoulder, PRINCE FELIX of the Fortunate Isles, disguised as TOM TUCKER, a travelling artisan.)

PRINCE. Ah! gentlemen of Gotham. Hail good day
Will fair day's work secure a fair day's pay?
I am a travelling workman, and can take
A share in anything you want to make.

RALPH. The very man; we're going to build a bowl.

PRINCE. Then I'll assist you with my heart and soul.

RICHARD. It's a big bowl, we are all here going to sea in it?

PRINCE. I see, it must have room enough for three in it.

RALPH. Wonderful man! I said how wise he looked.

PRINCE. Hammer, and wood, and nails, that job is booked.

ROBIN. He knows at once the very things to get.

RICHARD. I've never seen a workman like him yet.

PRINCE. *(Aside.)* They little know a prince is here before 'em.
Who loves the daughter of King Cockalorum;
Her picture put my heart in quite a pucker.

RALPH. Your name is?

PRINCE. Tom, my other name is Tucker.
Enough for dinner, work will always bring for it,-

RALPH, RICHARD, ROBIN. And how do you get your supper?

PRINCE. Bless you sing for it.

Song—"*Sedition Rondo*"

PRINCE.

I'M ONE WHO TAKES THE WORLD ABOUT ME
QUITE AS IT COMES, WITH ROSE OR THORN;
OF COURSE, IT MIGHT DO WELL WITHOUT ME,
JUST AS IT DID 'ERE I WAS BORN.
BUT, IF IN LIVES OF HONEST LABOUR,
ALL MEN DO THEIR BEST, I'M SURE
EVERY MAN MUST DO GOOD TO HIS NEIGHBOUR,
TILL ALL ARE BETTER OFF THAN BEFORE.
OFTEN WITH WORK TO BE DONE IN A HURRY,
PRINCES AND MONARCHS HAVE PLENTY OF WORRY,

So I've very often thought,
E'en honours may be dearly bought.

RALPH. Quite my opinion, Mr. Thomas Tucker.

RICHARD. You're just in time to come to our succour.

ROBIN. Here is our workshop, will it please you view it?

RALPH. You make the bowl, and we'll all see you do it.

PRINCE. You have a brook that turns a mill, however.

RALPH. Wheels, turned by water! Isn't water clever?

PRINCE. Well, come along, such work I understand,
And I'll soon turn this big bowl out of hand.

> *(Music. Three men take PRINCE into workshop. Change of
> Music "Laird of Cockpen" heard first softly as in the distance,
> then approaches nearer. VILLAGERS coining forward and
> intimating their delight at the advance of the KING and Court.
> Enter COCKALORUM the Great, King of Cockaigne, attended
> by Grand Chamberlain, Court Physician, Lord High Treasurer,
> Chief Justice, Chancellor of Exchequer, President of Council,
> Master of the Horse, Guards and Courtiers, the PRINCESS
> POPPET, of Cockaigne, attended by Nurse, Ladies in Waiting,
> and her retinue.)*

KING. Here will we on our royal progress rest,
And take refreshment as it seemeth best.
Now, rustics, since we've visited this spot,
We'll honour you by taking all you've got.
Your choicest wine our royal hearts will cheer,
While others may regale themselves on beer.

> *(Villagers refresh the Monarch with a flagon of wine, and
> distribute jugs of beer to attendants.)*

My temper's bad, the slightest things upset it,
I want my way in everything, and get it.
There's not a man in all my wide dominions,
About my meaning can have two opinions.
Or if he does, and daringly confesses it,
He rues the very moment he expresses it.

> *(Consternation of Villagers and Courtiers.)*

PRINCESS. Oh! what a stupid place.

KING. It is, my dear;

That was the reason why I brought you here.
Now don't you think it is a pity, rather,
My handsome child how very like your father!
You should be well, I'll mildly say
"A dunce."

PRINCESS. You might have said a fool, papa, at once,
You know I'm so like you.

KING. In face; for t'other
I trace a strong resemblance to your mother.

PRINCESS. That I am somewhat stupid, I admit,
I try to learn, but can't improve a bit.

KING. Can't you contrive to look a little wise?
Just shut your mouth, and open wide your eyes,
And something nice I think that I could send you,

PRINCESS. What's that, papa?

KING. A husband to attend you,
Who would with title give you wealth and lands,
And take a deal of trouble off my hands.

PRINCESS. What! let me have a nice new doll to play with,
Whose arms I might pull off and make away with?

KING. That which you wish to do, will please your lover,
That which you can't do, leave him to discover.
I want to hear some stupid man propose.

(Enter PRINCE FELIX from workshop.)

PRINCE. The bowl is finished, and away it goes.
(Bowl, with three men, seen launched.)
This wooden bowl, the fame of Gotham spreads,

RALPH. We three all made it out of our own heads.

PRINCE. *(Aside.)* There's the princess of whom I've seen the picture,
And in my heart have framed it as a fixture.
If she requires a husband, I'm the man.

KING. What means this bowl?

PRINCE. To go sire where it can.
In this big bowl three men are going to sea.

KING. What?

PRINCE. That's a secret sire, that rests with me.

KING. Adventurous men, who go on the deep water,
Proclaim that I have got a lovely daughter.
Whoe'er with common sense that girl provides,
Shall have her hand, my blessing, too, besides.

> (*The Men of Gotham accept the commission, and bowl works off.*)

PRINCE. From what I've heard, I think I know the plan.

KING. You do! Then tell it, there's a good young man.

Air—"Bay of Cherokee"

PRINCE.
THERE'S A STRANGE OLD TALE OF THE WONDERS TO BE SEEN
ON MIDSUMMER EVE OLD STYLE
BUT YOUR NERVES MUST BE STRONG, AND YOUR HEART BE TRUE,
AND YOUR CONSCIENCE DEVOID OF GUILE.
EVERY HUNDRED YEARS, ON THE NEIGHBOURING PLAIN,
ON THAT NIGHT THERE IS SAID TO BE,
IF YOU ONLY GO THERE AS THE CLOCK STRIKES TWELVE,
SUCH A FAIR AS WE OUGHT TO SEE.
IT'S A TALE YOU WON'T BELIEVE, BUT THEY TELL ME AT THE TIME,
AS MUSHROOMS RISE IN VIEW,
THAT A FAIR JUST FANCY IS HELD UPON THE GREEN,
BY SOME JOLLY LITTLE ELVES AND THEIR CREW.
I RECEIVED THE ACCOUNT FROM A VERY OLD MAN,
AGED MORE THAN A CENTURY;
HE WAS THERE THE VERY NIGHT, WHEN IT LAST DID OCCUR,
AND TO NIGHT IT AGAIN WILL BE.
IT'S THE VERY KIND OF TALE TO BE TOLD TO THE MARINES,
TALE OF THE GOOD OLD STYLE,
THO' OUR NERVES MAY BE STRONG, WHERE ARE HEARTS THAT
ARE TRUE,
WITH A CONSCIENCE DEVOID OF GUILE?

> (*The PRINCE takes the opportunity of showing his attachment to the PRINCESS. The KING interrupts their love making. The PRINCE indicates he is resolved to win the PRINCESS, and be at the midnight fair. COURT go off one side, and VILLAGERS the other.*)

SCENE II

Gotham Common on Midsummer Eve.

Enter, to Music, the PRINCE, who makes his way among the Mushrooms plentifully growing on the Common.

PRINCE. Well, here I am, the strangest of positions,
    I really think I answer all conditions.
    My nerves are strong, my conscience has no sting,
    And true as steel, the heart I have to bring.
    I won't turn back, whate'er comes in my way;
    Something advances, who are you, I say?

    (Music. Enter the Fairy ELFINA disguised as Old Woman, with crutch.)

ELFINA. A poor old dame who only comes in sight,
    To gather mushrooms growing here to-night.

PRINCE. Let me assist you, ah! confound the pins.

    (Smarting under effect of touch as he supports her arm.)

ELFINA. Wasn't it conscience pricked you for your sins?
    Aren't you afraid, young man, whoe'er you be,
    To trust yourself here, all alone with me?

PRINCE. I know no guile, ne'er meant one any harm.

ELFINA. If so, then you're the chap to work the charm,
    Something, if you look round you circumspectly,
    Out of the common you will see directly.
    Listen! I think it is about the time.

    (Village dock strikes twelve.)

PRINCE. The clock strikes twelve.

ELFINA. When ends that midnight chime
    Observe these mushrooms, what there now appears
    No one has witnessed for a hundred years.
    (Mysterious Music. Piano.)
    Look there! Behold!

    (Movement of Mushrooms.)

PRINCE. The mushrooms up are springing,
    And something odd from underground are bringing.

ELFINA. You see at present everywhere among us,
    A mushroom, popularly called a fungus.
    I do but strike my crutch, and with this plunge, I
    Reveal the funny figures of the Fungi.
    They get no higher wages than my thanks,

Yet here they are, with all their pretty pranks.

(ELFINA strikes crutch, which she throws off with her disguise! Mushrooms go through evolutions.)

They have a wholesome reputation got,
Not like these toadstools, who are an awful lot.

(Dance of toadstools.)

More quickly now than mushrooms here will grow,
The Fairies' Fancy Fair and Flower Show.

(Rapid change to—)

SCENE III

The Fairies' Fancy Fair and Flower Show.

Transformation of Mushrooms to the stalls at which Fairies preside. Rapid movements of the glittering elves, &c. The stage presents a general scene of animation till ELFINA speaks.

ELFINA. *(To PRINCE.)* Look round you;
    Here may favoured mortals buy
    Whatever article most charms the eye.
    Offer no money, coin no fairies take,
    With gentle words and looks the purchase make.

PRINCE. Thanks for the hint, my bargain seems a rare one,
    What pretty toy will please my simple fair one?
    What shall I buy for her?

(FAIRIES at stalls invite custom.)

IST FAIRY. A bunch of flowers.
    A choice bouquet fresh culled from beauty's bowers.

2ND FAIRY. A feather brush removes each trace of care.
    find there's nothing prettier in the fair.

3RD FAIRY. Some rare old tapestry, quite free from fracture,
    Warranted real Goblin manufacture.

4TH FAIRY. Six articles entirely useless. These
    Are most expensive, and are sure to please.

5TH FAIRY. Pincushions fashioned in all kinds of forms.

6TH FAIRY. A glass foretelling matrimonial storms.

7TH FAIRY. Portraits of public men who hold high places,

A famous chance to recognise their faces.

8TH FAIRY. The likenesses of those, both long and deeply
Engaged on a late trial going cheaply.

9TH FAIRY. Some curious witnesses for the accused,
No reasonable offer now refused.

PRINCE. I have opinions not quite orthodox,
So choose instead this simple Jack in Box.
A more ingenious toy man ne'er devised,
You know what's coming but are still surprised.
Now-a-days, folks seem scarce surprised at all,
"Jack in the Box," I take you from the stall.

> *(Music. PRINCE receives from stall a box, a large imitation of a toy labelled "Jack in the Box" and places it on stage.)*

ELFINA. No wiser choice could mortal man have made,
Here lies our cleverest sprite in ambuscade,
A curious Elf, who everyone surprises.

PRINCE. I touch the spring, then pop, and up he rises.
> *(Music. Appearance of JACK IN THE Box.)*
This is the strangest toy man ever bought.

JACK. Want me? and Jack springs up as quick as thought.
I'm double-jointed, light as clouds ethereal,
And warranted well made, of best material.

> *(Music. JACK illustrates his elasticity by a series of movements.)*

ELFINA. You have become his master from to-day,
What you command, lie swiftly will obey.

JACK. Just such a faithful servant rail I make you.

PRINCE. You will! Then, as your owner, off I take you.
I'll see you to a fair Princess consigned,
Of faultless form, but undeveloped mind.
About the palace you shall antics play,
She may grow wiser thro' your pranks; away !

> *(Music. JACK expresses his devotion, and goes off with PRINCE.)*

ELFINA. Last chance to-night! what other youth appears?
Once only once in every hundred years.

Song—"The Fairies' Fancy Fair"

COME, WHO WILL HAVE THIS MAGIC SPELL,
I HAVE CHARMS FOR EVERY CARE,
YET, NOT FOR SILVER FAIRIES SELL,
SO BUYERS MUST BEWARE.
NOR TAKE WE GOLD FOR WHAT IS SOLD,
BUT A LOOK FROM A LOVING EYE,
AND A GENTLE WORD IN THE TWILIGHT HEARD,
WILL PRICELESS TREASURES BUY.
THEN MORTALS ALL, COME ROUND MY STALL,
HERE NO ONE NEED DESPAIR,
YOU GET WITH A GLANCE, THE LUCKIEST CHANCE,
AT THE FAIRIES' FANCY FAIR.
THIS FAIRY CHARM IS REALLY CHEAP,
WHEN ROUND THE NECK 'TIS HUNG,
ALL THOSE WHO WEAR THE LOCKET, KEEP
THEIR HEARTS FOR EVER YOUNG.
IT HOLDS YOU TRUE TO THE ONE YOU KNEW,
IN THE BRIGHTEST DAYS OF YORE,
AND IT BRINGS YOU BACK, BY A ROSY TRACK,
TO THE HAPPY OLD TIMES ONCE MORE.
BUT MORTALS ALL, AT EVERY STALL,
WHEN HITHER YOU REPAIR,
HEARTS MUST NOT RANGE, WE HAVE NEVER CHANGE
AT THE FAIRIES' FANCY FAIR.

GRAND TABLEAU

BALLET

(On which scene changes to—)

SCENE IV

The Cabinet of King Cockalorum.

Quick Pantomime Music, and enter rapidly KING, driving before him all his Ministers, Courtiers, &c., and followed by Guards who range at back.

KING. Don't talk to me I'm savage, and I know it;
When I am in a rage I let you know it.
Groom of the Bedchamber

(Trembling ATTENDANT advances.)

I gave you warning,
My royal razor wasn't stropped this morning.
Confine the caitiff fifty fathoms deep

In lowest dungeon of the castle keep.
Where's the First Lord in Waiting?

(FIRST LORD advances nervously as GROOM exits.)

Sir, I found
My toast this morning blacked instead of browned
For this, until I hear of due repentance,
Twelve months in banishment shall be your sentence.
Clerk of the Kitchen—

(CLERK advances with trembling knees.)

Didn't I this minute
Discover gravy with a cinder in it I
This is contempt of Court it does amaze me !
Fine him a thousand pounds, and see he pays me.

Air—"King and Countryman"

THE MONARCH I AM OF A WIDE DOMAIN,
I'M KING OF THE COUNTRY CALLED COCKAIGNE.
I'LL HAVE MY OWN WAY AS LONG AS I REIGN,
AND AFTER I'VE DONE I SHALL WANT IT AGAIN;
AS THE RIGHTFUL HEIR ALL, ONE TO SHARE ALL,
EMPEROR OF COCKAIGNE.
A DAUGHTER I HAVE SO DULL AND DENSE,
SHE HASN'T THE SMALLEST GRAIN OF SENSE,
AND THE STUPIDEST FOLKS I FOUND, WERE HENCE
TOO WISE TO HAVE HER ON ANY PRETENCE.
AS I MADE MY RURAL, TOUR ALL, CURE ALL,
AGONY OF SUSPENSE.
SO HERE I AM, ON MY FORMER TRACK,
AND NOT IN THE BEST OF TEMPERS, BACK;
OF SUITORS HERE IF I FIND A LACK,
I CAN ONLY SAY THERE WILL BE A WHACK.
FA-LARAL, SHARE ALL, MAKING YOU CARE ALL
WHACKETTY, RACKETTY, CRACK.

KING. Where is my daughter? don't you see I'm calm?
Where is my daugh—? you needn't feel alarm.
Where is my daughter? Why do you not reply?
Go off, or else your heads will by-and-by.

(Enter NURSE, with Lady in Waiting.)

Oh! here is one, who from her situation,

Ought to possess a little information.
Where's the princess, immediately away to her,
State that her father has a word to say to her.

LADY IN WAITING. There! don't you hear, nurse ?
Why don't you obey?
Great Cockalorum has a word to say.

(Exit NURSE.)

KING. A word! I shall want hundreds ere I've done.
(Enter PRINCESS POPPET.)
Oh! here you are, you precious simpleton!
You know I'm anxious, girl, you should be married,
Ere by some revolution off I'm carried.
Such things have been and may be once again,
If you were wedded, you might hope to reign.

PRINCESS. But I'm so stupid I should not know how.

KING. That's no objection, government rules now.
You only sit, and nod, and say
"All right!"
I've reigned so many a year.

PRINCESS. Seems easy, quite.

KING. Of course it is, but in the wedded state,
A man requires an intellectual mate.
I don't expect you to have brains like Plato's,
But you might learn to well, say, boil potatoes.

PRINCESS. Do you believe in fairies, pa ?

KING. No, pooh!

PRINCESS. I didn't once, but now I think I do.
I had a dream last night, and during sleep
They gave me such a pretty toy to keep.
With that, my education seemed completed,
And fairies said—

KING. You're always so conceited
You think because you're pretty, that's enough,
You'll find it isn't.

PRINCESS. Fairies said that

KING. Stuff!
I'll hear no more. As princely suitors rose up
And asked your hand, you turned your pretty nose up.

And now I've travelled the whole country thro',
No lord seems fool enough to look at you.

(Enter HERALD with Trumpet?)

HERALD. Sire, I'm desired

KING. You are, to quickly tell

HERALD. A handsome stranger has arrived.

KING. 'Tis well.
Admit him to our royal presence. Stay!
What ho! Blow there, trumpets blow away.

(Exit HERALD. Vehement flourish of trumpeted.)

By that, the stranger waiting for admission
Will know we are in a flourishing condition.
Now leave each syllable to your papa,
And don't reveal the silly belle you are.

(Lively music. Enter PRINCE FELIX, still disguised as TOM TUCKER, with "Jack in the Box.")

PRINCE. Fair lady, mighty monarch, here you see
One of good name, tho' not of high degree.
(To PRINCESS.) I know you're pretty, I have heard you're proud,
Yet hope my presents here may be allowed.

PRINCESS. And you have brought ?

PRINCE. *(Presents Jack in Box.)* This gift.

PRINCESS. Oh ! I shall scream!
The youth and toy I pictured in my dream.

KING. It seems a curious sort of thing.

PRINCE. You'll say so,
For when I touch this spring he pops away so.

(Rapid music. Disappearance and Re-appearance of JACK, to the bewilderment of KING and Court, who vainly try to catch him.)

PRINCE. You see this Jack in Box which I have brought,
Is not a man that's easy to be caught.

KING. Wonderful, really! perfect to each particle,
What shall we say for this ingenious article?

PRINCE. Your daughter's hand.

KING. Agreed so let it be.

PRINCESS. This person isn't good enough for me.
Altho' I own the toy is most complete.

PRINCE. *(Aside.)* 'Ere long we'll find a cure for this conceit.
(Aloud.) I offer you Princess, a deep affection,
(Aside.) And undertake your faults shall find correction.
(Aloud.) Observe, your common toy can only squeak,
This is a Jack who'll dance, and sing, and speak.

KING. Capital notion; Jack with joints and jerks,
I'll make you Chairman of our Board of Works.

PRINCE. Law Courts unbuilt would then not long remain.

JACK. Just so in, out, here, there, and back again.

(JACK illustrates the swiftness of his movements by a specimen of its activity before the KING.)

Air—"Madame Angot"

PRINCE.
THO' HUMBLE IN MY CALLING,
UNBLEMISHED IS MY NAME,
LET THIS EXCUSE MY FALLING
IN LOVE WITH ONE OF FAME ;
UNTITLED THO' YOU TAKE HIM,
A YOUTH OF LOWLY LIFE,
HE DARES TO THINK YOU'LL MAKE HIM
WELL SUITED WITH A WIFE.
JACK IFF THE BOX. 27'
FORTUNE FAVOURING,
YOU NOT WAVERING,
HERE A HUSBAND YOU BEHOLD ;
DON'T MIND TRINKETS,
DON'T YOU THINK IT'S
BETTTER TO HAVE LOVE THAN GOLD.

Air—"I Should Like To"

KING.
I SHOULD LIKE TO. I SHOULD LIKE TO.
I HOPE THAT SHE WILL NOT SAY "SHAN'T."
BUT A BRIDE, TOO, I HAVE TRIED TO
LONG MARRY HER OFF BUT I CAN'T.

Air—"I Wish I Was"

KING.
I'M NOT SATISFIED AT ALL

WITH WHAT SHE IS, BUT COULD
I ONLY MAKE HER SOMETHING ELSE
I VERY QUICKLY WOULD.

PRINCE.

I MADLY AM IN LOVE,
AS DEEP AS MAN CAN BE;
BUT SUCH CONCEIT I NEVER DID MEET,
AS HERE I CHANCE TO SEE.
I WISH IT WAS TO BE;
BUT HER LIPS, THO' SWEET AS HONEY,
ARE UNDER A NOSE THAT TURNS UP
AT EVERY MAN WITH MONEY.
I WISH SHE WAS AGAIN
AT HER SCHOOL, WHERE SHE SHOULD BE;
I WISH SHE HAD A GRAIN OF SENSE,
THEN SHE WOULD MARRY ME.

Air—"Evans' Pantmimical"

JACK.

PECULIAR THING THE PRINCESS IS,
SO IMPUDENT A "CUSS;"
BUT IF YOU ONLY WAIT AWHILE,
YOU NEEDN'T MAKE A FUSS,
I KNOW A PLAN TO WORK A CURE,
YOU LEAVE IT ALL TO US.
HIXTUM, STIXTUM, YOU SHALL SEE
HER PRIDE SHALL GO DOWN PLUMP.
JUST TOUCH MY SPRING, ENOUGH FOR ME,
HOW I WILL MAKE HER JUMP!
OH DEAR! OH LAW!
FOR I AM JACK IN THE BOX!

CHORUS OF OTHERS

HIXTUM, STIXTUM, YOU WILL SEE
HER PRIDE SHALL GO DOWN PLUMP.
JUST TOUCH HIS SPRING, AND QUICKLY HE
WILL MAKE THE PRINCESS JUMP !
OH DEAR! OH LAW!
FOR HE IS JACK IN THE BOX!

(PRINCESS conceitedly goes off and rest follow, dancing off to end of tune. Scene discovers—)

SCENE V

Court of the King of Cockaigne.

All the MINISTERS discovered round the throne. Enter KING, PRINCE FELIX, Guards, etc. KING ascends throne with marked ceremony.

KING. Here, in possession of our royal chair,
　　　　Let Cockalorum settle this affair.
　　　　In vain to coax his child your monarch tries.
　　　　Can anybody anything advise?
　　　　As peacock proud, she's obstinate as mule.

IRISH MAN. Shure, don't you see what's wanted? Its "Home Rule."

KING. Silence!

IRISH MAN. Home rule it plainest common sense is.
　　　　We'll do the governing, you pay the expenses.

KING. Silence for Thomas Tucker!

PRINCE. Sire, I press
　　　　My suit as suitor to the fair Princess.
　　　　The picture of her beauty I must say
　　　　Fell short of that which I beheld to-day;
　　　　And as the fair original does exceed
　　　　All that the artist painted her, indeed
　　　　So do my feeble words but faintly show
　　　　A depth of love much more than she can know.

KING. Sensibly spoken like a good young man.
　　　　Now Thomas Tucker, if you'll find a plan
　　　　To cure her great conceit and dense stupidity,
　　　　Why you shall marry her.

　　　　　　(MINISTERS bow assent.)

PRINCE. Done, Sire. With rapidity
　　　　Let the Princess appear ; with help of Jack
　　　　The lady to her senses I'll bring back.

KING. Call the Princess! This matter we will wind up.
　　　　　　(Enter PRINCESS, NURSE, LADIES.)
　　　　Now, Madam, have you made your little mind up ?

PRINCESS. Not I. The fair Princess of these dominions
　　　　Has of herself the highest of opinions?

PRINCE. Then Jack in Box spring up. The name I call

Can make the greatest of them here feel small!

(JACK IN Box appears.)

JACK. Behold me! The Princess, as small Bo-Peep,
Will lose her subjects, all transformed to sheep.
King of Cockaigne, Jack Homer you become ;
Be a good boy and you'll pick out the plum.
Reduced in size when I one touch bestow,
Away to Nursery Island all must go.

(KING descends throne. Alarm of Court.)

Air—"Eaton Square"

KING.

OH! THIS SORT OF THING IS ALL VERY WELL,
BUT I THINK IT ISN'T FAIR;
WHEN YOU HAVE A MIND TO BE A SWELL,
TO BE PACKED OFF ANYWHERE.

Air—"Have You Seen the Shah?"

PRINCE.

YOU'LL SEE WHAT YOU ARE BOYS YOU'LL SEE WHAT YOU ARE,
WHEN YOU ARE SENT TO NURSERY LAND, WHICH IS PECULIAR.
STUCK UP WITH PRIDE, YOU WOULD DERIDE THE WISH OF
    YOUR PAPA,
AND ONLY ANSWER EVERYONE WITH "PSHA!"

Air—"Belle of the Ball"

WHEN YOU'RE SMALL YOU ARE ALWAYS DELIGHTED
AT GETTING SOME FUN ON THE CHANCE;
BUT THERE'S NOTHING WITH WHICH YOU'RE REQUITED,
IN YEARS AS YOU COME TO ADVANCE.
MEN REMAIN ONLY BENT ON GAIN
AND GIRLS ARE BENT UPON BEAUX
WHILE YOU ALL ARE FORGETTING THE TRUTHS
THAT FROM NURSERY ISLAND AROSE.
AND SO WE MUST ALL BE SMALL, DEAR BOYS,
AND SO WE MUST ALL BE SMALL, DEAR BOYS;
TILL WE OUR FAULTS CAN RECALL, DEAR BOYS,
WE MUST BE ALL OF US SMALL.

(JACK, during chorus, touches each of the characters, and by the time the air has ended the transformation is effected. The KING, PRINCE, PRINCESS, and all the Court have disappeared, and in their places are LITTLE BO-PEEP, with crook, TOM TUCKER, JACK HORNER, with pie, PETER PIPER, picking his peck of pepper; Baker's Man, with cake, MARGERY DAW, with see-saw; and JACK SPRATT and WIFE, HUMPTY DUMPTY, LITTLE MISS MUFFETT, SIMPLE SIMON, and LITTLE BOY BLUE, in background. Tableau. JACK IN THE Box points triumphantly to the result of the change he has effected, and as he goes off the characters become animated.)

TOM T. Jack in the Box his purpose has made plain,
We are all sent back to childhood's days again.

BO-PEEP. Where am I? Wasn't I once a great Princess?
And isn't that my father only less?

TOM T. Yes, that's the monarch seated in the corner.
His kingdom is a pie, his name Jack Horner.

BO-PEEP. Our Chancellor of Exchequer see there sticking!

TOM T. Now Peter Piper pecks of pepper picking.

BO-PEEP. And there our Lord Chief Justice, by see-saw,
Keeping the proper balance of the law.
That Baker's Man, who pricks a name with holes?

TOM T. Now Pat-a-Cake, once Master of the Rolls.

BO-PEEP. My Ladies of the Court, where shall I find them ?

TOM T. They're sheep, and awful tales have left behind them.

BO-PEEP. Oh, what a change! Most curious it does seem.
When shall I hear of them?

TOM T. In Bo-Peep's dream.

(Slow music. TOM TUCKER waves his hand; characters disperse, and scene changes to—)

SCENE VI

Nursery Island.

Lively Pastoral Music, as scene opens. Enter CHILDREN gathering buttercups and daisies. Appearance of the missing sheep passes in succession. When they have gone off, BO-PEEP enters, meeting TOM TUCKER.

BO-PEEP. Oh, Thomas Tucker what a lucky meeting,
    I've lost my sheep, but dreamed I heard them bleating;
    By hook or crook I'm quite resolved to find them,

TOM T. Leave them alone no tales they'll leave behind them.
    But now no more seems Thomas Tucker chid.

BO-PEEP. I feel so different from what I did,
    No longer I'm conceited.

TOM T. Well I never!

BO-PEEP. I've grown, too, much more sensible and clever.
    My nursery playmates with attention honour me,
    Jack Sprat has taught me lessons in economy.
    Patience from Peter Piper have I learned,
    And Simple Simon, how a penny's turned.

TOM T. While Humpty Dumpty tumbling from the wall,
    Has warned you of the danger of a fall.

BO-PEEP. Nay I have been industrious too, you know,
    Little Miss Muffet taught me how to sew.
    And when I said at music I would try,
    Little Boy Blew his horn, and so could I.

TOM T. Why, thus endowed, you'll lead a useful life,
    And I would marry had I such a wife.

BO-PEEP. Then you shall be my little sweetheart still.

TOM T. Most charming of small mortals, so I will;

BO-PEEP. Here is my fortune I am rich in wool,
    (Black sheep crosses with three bags.)
    Three bags you see, and every bag is full.
    One for Papa, once Emperor of Cockaigne,
    Two for provisions going down Ked Lane.

TOM T. Why we are rich, indeed; this reformation
    Will soon make all resume their former station.

Air—"Down by the Old Mill Stream"

BO-PEEP.
    IF YOU WOULD BE CONTENTED AS A FARMER,
    I SHOULD BE ALSO BLEST.

QUITE SURE THAT YOU LIKED YOUR LITTLE CHARMER,
IF ONLY SHE TRIED TO DO HER BEST.
THE HUMBLEST FARE, SHE'D GLADLY SHARE,
NO FROWN SHOULD E'ER BE SEEN,
YOU'LL NOT FORGET YOUR CHARMING LITTLE PET,
YOU MET UPON BUTTERCUP GREEN.
REFRAIN.
YES, UPON BUTTERCUP GREEN,
MANY HAPPY HOURS SHALL BE SEEN.
DANCING EVERY DAY, WE'LL PASS THE HOURS AWAY,
LIVING UPON BUTTERCUP GREEN.

(Fandango, and Ballet of Buttercups and Daisies. On which scene closes—)

SCENE VII

The Broken Bowl on the Black Rocks.

Marked Music. Enter with their quarter staves, RALPH, RICHARD, and ROBIN, the Three Wise Men of Gotham.

RALPH. Alas! we're wrecked, but had our bowl been stronger,
No doubt our story would have been much longer.

RICHARD. Our voyage has been short, but still, dear brother,
It will be long before I make another.

ROBIN. Cast on these rocks, it useless is complaining,
Let's make the best of all the staves remaining.

(The three confer at side, while enter—as invisible—on the oilier side, ELFINA, HARMONICA, and attendants.)

HARMONICA. Behold, my fairy queen, here are the three
Wise men of Gotham, who went forth to sea.
Jack in the Box that toy the mortal bought,
Has to her senses Princess Poppet brought.
And long imprisoned fays can cleave the air,
Freed by the produce of the Fancy Fair.

RALPH. At least, if we get back to Gotham Green,
No one more stupid than ourselves we've seen.

(They range in line with Fairies.)

Air—Conspirator's Chorus "Madame Angot"

WHEN FOLKS DO WRONG, WHICH THEY'D BETTER NOT,
AND CHOOSE TO SAY IT'S A WAY THEY'VE GOT,
THE WISEST COURSE THEY CAN PURSUE,
IS NO SUCH THING AGAIN TO DO.

ELFINA. Men talking in so sensible a strain,
Fairies shall see you safely home again.

RALPH. Fairies!

HARMONICA. Well, yes, that power you may perceive in us,
It's only men of science don't believe in us.

ELFINA. Make yourselves visible to mortal eyes,
See, who comes here arrayed in princely guise.

HARMON. The very one How strangely things befall!
Who Jack in Box selected from my stall.

(Enter PRINCE FELIX, handsomely attired.)

PRINCE. Regaining figure, I resume my style,
Once more Prince Felix of the Fortunate Isle.
But where's my pretty wife who charmed my eyes,
Improved in mind tho' much reduced in size.

HARMON. 'Twas I who sold the toy to work the cure.

PRINCE. And honestly I purchased it, I'm sure.
(Assent of Fairies.)
I'm changed from Thomas Tucker, I confess,
But where's Bo-Peep, my beautiful Princess?
Has Jack in Box betrayed me after all,
Restored my form, and kept the Princess small!

HARMON. It may be so. Jack curious tricks will play.

PRINCE. And so, malicious fairy, that's your way.

Air—Quarrel Duo "Madame Angot"

PRINCE and **HARMONICA**.
AH ! NOW I SEE THE REASON WHY
THAT FAIRY CHARMS ARE BAD TO BUY.
THEY VERY TEMPTINGLY APPEAR,
BUT BREAK THE PROMISE TO THE EAR.
OH ! WHY THE STORY DID I TRUST,
IF ONE COULD DO IT THAT I MUST.
WELL, YOU HAVE HAD YOUR FANCY FAIR,
AND TO REPEAT IT NEVER DARE.
FOR I WILL TELL THE WORLD WITHOUT,

WHAT WICKED THINGS YOU ARE ABOUT.
A SIMPLE
"THANK YOU!" IS YOUR PRICE,
IT ISN'T DEAR, AND VERY NICE.
BUT WHEN WE BUY, THE PURCHASE IS BUT NOUGHT,
AND MORTAL MAN IS THEN TO RUIN BROUGHT.

OMNES.
OH! DON'T HE SCOLD THE OTHER,
WHAT MAKES HIM GO ON SO?
HE'LL NEVER BUY ANOTHER
FAIRY CHARM, WE KNOW.

HARMONICA.
AH ! NOW YOU SEE THE REASON WHY
THOSE FAIRY CHARMS YOU HAD TO BUY.
OF COURSE THEY TEMPTINGLY APPEAR,
AND BREAK THE PROMISE TO THE EAR.
OH! WHY THE STORY DID YOU TRUST,
AND THINK TO DO IT THAT YOU MUST.
YES, WE HAVE HAD OUR FANCY FAIR,
AND TO REPEAT IT SOON WILL DARE.
THO' YOU MAY TELL THE WORLD WITHOUT
WHAT WICKED THINGS WE ARE ABOUT.
A SIMPLE "THANK YOU!" IS OUR PRICE,
IT ISN'T DEAR FOR WHAT IS NICE.
BUT WHEN YOU BUY, THIS LESSON SHOULD BE TAUGHT.
YOU SHOULD TAKE CARE OF THAT WHICH YOU HAVE BOUGHT.

OMNES.
OH! DON'T SHE SCOLD THE OTHER,
WHAT MAKES HER GO ON SO?
HE'LL NEVER BUY ANOTHER
FAIRY CHARM, WE KNOW.

ELFINA. Cease these disputes, Jack truly worked his spell,
For here come all the rest restored as well.

(Enter KING and PRINCESS.)

PRINCESS. Good gracious, Tom, do you turn out a Prince?
I'm greatly changed, and better ever since.

KING. Bless you. my child no, that's been said before,
King of Cockaigne, a crow would suit you more.

(KING gives his own Royal Flourish.)

PRINCE. Jack in the Box, this lesson plainly taught:

"Happiness means simplicity of thought.
Teaching conceit and ignorance are allies,
And even nursery tales may make us wise."

(Lively dance of characters off. Then stage darkened, and DARK FAIRY appears, liberated from captivity by the result of the sympathetic purchase of the Fancy Fair. Testifies her delight by a fantastic dance, at end of which scene changes to—)

SCENE VIII

The golden land of plenty harvest home of the fairies.

The FAIRY CORNUCOPIA advances.

FAIRY. Here where old Time speeds on with rapid wing,
Welcome to all with every friend you bring.
Plenty we hope to see on every side,
Plenty of mirth these funny folks provide.

HARLEQUINADE COMMENCES

END

CINDERELLA

or

Harlequin and the Fairy slipper

❧❧

(1878)

Cinderella was first presented on December 26, 1878 at the Drury Lane with the following cast:

Baron Pumpernickel................... Frederick Vokes

Kobold, his Trusty Servant............. Fawdon Vokes

Ella, surnamed "Cinderella"............ Victoria Vokes

Vixena, the Spiteful, her Sister........ Miss Hudspeth

Pavonia, the Proud, her Sister......... Julia Warden

Azor, the Poodle...................... Master Cullen

Prince Amabel......................... Jessie Vokes

Wizewitz, the Prince's Tutor.......... Mr. Barsby

Bizarre, the Prince's Page............. Miss Nott

Iris, the Spirit of the Rainbow......... Sallie Sinclair

SCENE 1

Mountain Pass and Woody Glen in the Black Forest, by Sunset.

A solitary tree, P.S. Charcoal-burners' hut opposite side. Wild Boars discovered enjoying themselves after their own boorish fashion. Horn heard in distance. Change of music, and alarm of Boars at the approach of huntsmen. They retreat gradually in opposite directions. Rapid music. a wild Boar enters, as if closely pursued. Looks eagerly about him, and ultimately takes refuge behind tree, occasionally peeping forth to watch proceedings. Marked music. Enter the BARON PUMPERNICKEL in hunting-dress, with spear, soon after followed by KOBOLD, his servant, with basket containing wine and provisions. They advance to front.

BARON. I am here again, and at the same old spot, too.
    Now where on earth can that old Boar have got to!
    Kobold, you are not afraid?

KOBOLD. *(Trembling.)* Afraid! no, master!
    Let the Boar run, you'll see who runs the faster.

BARON. Some Burgundy! A draught of wine will cheer me.
    Are you quite certain that no Boar is near me?

KOBOLD. *(Melodramatically.)* Sure!

BARON. What a roar! Boar's tusks are not my choice.

KOBOLD. 'Twas only me!

BARON. Then change that husky voice.
    What will you bet I slay him on the spot?

KOBOLD. I'll lay a tablecloth—that's all I've got.
    (Lays tablecloth accordingly. KOBOLD puts basket near trunk of tree, and Boar rapidly appropriates the provisions, while BARON drinks his wine.)
    Of that same German sausage let's avail ourselves,
    And being near to Spears and Pond, regale ourselves.

    (KOBOLD goes to basket, which he finds emptied.)

KOBOLD. Oh, master, master! We are fairly quit of it,
    Somebody's been and swallowed every bit of it.

BARON. My sausage gone! Search everywhere, and find it.

KOBOLD. That tree conceals a Boar, Sir! Look behind it.

    (Music. Dispute between BARON and his servant as to which shall go first. Business between BARON and the Boar.)

BARON. To silence Boards, one should have lots of leisure.

Attack him!

KOBOLD. Yes, Sir! After you, with pleasure.

Air—"Hi Cockalorum"

BARON.

OLD COCKALORUM FIERCE AND BIG,
JIG, JIG, JIG! AWFUL PIG!
WE CAN SEE YOU BEHIND THAT TWIG,
OLD COCKALORUM.
JIG, JIG, JIG!

(Waltz Melody.)

WE'LL PUT A LEMON IN YOUR MOUTH,
AND MAKE YOU PRETTY LOOK,
AND INTRODUCE YOU TO A GENTLE.
MAN WE CALL THE COOK.

> *(More business between the BARON and the Boar, ending by the latter throwing his two pursers to the ground, and getting safely away.)*

BARON. Gone off with all my luncheon, and the rest of it,
I am much afraid we didn't get the best of it.
> *(Horns heard without.)*
More horns, and blown with lungs so sound and hearty,
Why this must be the Prince's hunting party.

> *(Hunting music. The Prince's retainers enter, some bearing the spoils of the chase. Then WISEWITZ the Prince's tutor; finally, PRINCE AMABEL, followed by his page BIZARRE. PRINCE and his TUTOR encounter BARON and KOBOLD in centre.)*

PRINCE. No wonder such small port we have had to-day,
These frights have scared our noble game away.

BARON. Begging your pardon, your serenest highness,
The Boars are not afflicted with such shyness.
Six thousand Boars already have I slain,
And not much more than three alive remain.

PRINCE. If that be true, no logic can confute it;
Even my tutor, Wisewitz, won't dispute it.
Here will we pause, and take a slight repast.

BARON. Thank goodness! Dinner-time has come at last.

(Lively Music. Retainers prepare picnic and unload hampers. One seen visibly holding knives and forks.)

PRINCE. Here we have herbs of all sorts, and some curry.

WISE. We have verbs and various kinds--see Lindley Murray.

PRINCE. Come spread the cloth, and be of plates collective.

WISE. As Regular, Irregular, and Defective.

PRINCE. Don't down my throat of grammar be a stuffer.

WISE. Auxiliaries "To be," "To do," "To suffer."

(PRINCE thrusts aside WISEWITZ, who in his turn knocks BARON into hamper, where the knives and forks have been inconveniently packed perpendicularly. BARON rescued by his servant KOBOLD.)

PRINCE. There, no more lessons if you please at present.

WISE. Conjunctions are of two kinds.

BARON. One's unpleasant.

PRINCE. All in this case concerned are quite agreed,
Retainers need refreshers--so proceed,
Unpack the hamper! out with knives and forks.
Produce the bottles and let fly the corks.
While bachelors so light a load can carry,
Behold a Prince resolved to never marry.

(Music. Preparations for luncheon, and business of dividing contents of hampers, in which BARON and KOBOLD take the greatest interest. Enter from charcoal-burners' hut IRIS, the fairy, disguised as old woman in cloak, etc.)

IRIS. *(Aside.)* So mortals here. Their charity I'll try.
(Aloud.) Give a poor dame a crust of bread.

BARON. (Speaking with his mouth full.) Not I!
Why don't you work like me? See how I labour.

PRINCE. Here, take a share of what we have, good neighbour.
(Gives IRIS basket and purse.)
Within you'll find a trifle you may need
To-morrow morn some other mouths to feed.

IRIS. My heartfelt thanks, good Sir! You soon shall see
A prize and punishment bestowed by me.

(Exit IRIS into hut.)

PRINCE. Strange being that!

BARON. I thought the very same.

PRINCE. Haven't the pleasure, Sir, to know your name,
But please to fill your glass. To all a greeting.
A bumper toast to our next merry meeting.

WISE. Your royal highness, when you are quite at leisure,
Allow me just—

PRINCE. Another glass? with pleasure.

WISE. I mean, your highness seems to quite forget
We haven't done our mathematics yet.

PRINCE. That lively kind of game next week we'll play,
I mean to take a holiday to-day.
But bless me! These strong wines possess rare merits,
Their potent influence quite o'er comes my spirits.

BARON. I fancy that a nap would do me good.

PRINCE. I really shouldn't wonder if it would.

WISE. His royal highness here will take a doze.

PRINCE. Be forty winks the limit of repose.

*(Music. PRINCE reposes on bank. Retainers assuming
picturesque positions at back. Stage darkens.)*

Air—"Where was Moses"

BARON.
See he dozes after camping out,
Who supposes now what I'm about?
I'm the sort of man, when I find a can,
There my nose is, if the wine isn't out.

*(BARON and savants industriously empty all the cans and
bottles, and then betake themselves to rest uncomfortable near
the charcoal-burners' fire.)*

BARON. This sleeping out from one's own cost attics
Is awfully suggestive of rheumatics.

*(BARON at last reposes. Fairy music. IRIS appears in her own
form.)*

IRIS. Waft with your wings soft fancies through his brain,
Till love enthroned within his heart shall reign.

So fair a face the Prince's heart must fill;
Dreaming or waking, it must haunt him still.

(THE VISION, in which the face of CINDERELLA appears.)

CINDERELLA. This wish I utter to the powers above me,
All that I want is somebody to love me.

(Vision disappears. PRINCE awakens. All rise.)

PRINCE. Give me another nap. Bind up my eyes.
Such dreams from indigestion don't arise;
Nor does that malady in hearts cause pain.
Wake me not yet! Oh, let me dream again!

BARON. He must have had the nightmare—now, methinks,
A thousand joys derive from forty winks.

PRINCE. Here, Wisewitz—cause to shake your stupid head,
Or else a lesson I'll give you instead
Tell me my sentence. Did you see her face?

WISE. Feminine Gender! Nominative Case,
And must agree with—

PRINCE. Pshaw! Fly quickly hence!

BARON. I run.

WISE. You run. Verb active. Present tense.

PRINCE. Go! skim the beautiful, and scour the plain!
My kingdom to behold that face again.
To-morrow night your Prince will give a ball,
To find that girl who holds his heart in thrall;
To all his subjects he sends invitations.

BARON. Tell everyone to come with their relations.

PRINCE. Here's gold for him who swiftly stirs his pegs,
The largest bounty for the longest legs.
Send special messengers to every nation,
Spare no expense, nor fear remuneration.
Outstrip the wind! Nay, each one travel faster,
Or you'll be taught to dance without a master.

(Charcoal-burners enter.)

Air—"Brannigan's Band"

OMNES.

> QUICK MARCH! GIRLS ARCH, FIGURES THAT WILL STRIKE,
> FIND ME! WHO'S SHE? I SEEM TO ONCE TO LIKE,
> GO AND TRY, WHO'LL SUPPLY, THE FAIREST IN THE LAND,
> AND WHEN YOU'RE GONE, JUST THINK UPON THE PRINCE WHO
> OFFERS HIS HAND.

> *(Dance off. IRIS remaining to change scene.)*

SCENE II

The Glass Factory of the Fairy Slipper, in the Basaltic Valley.

Industrial movements of the Glass Goblins. IRIS, as Spirit of the Rainbow, greets her Attendants SILICA, CRYSTAL, SPARKLE, and ALUMINA.

IRIS. I am glad to see a scene of such activity,
> Your work shall soon be followed by festivity.
> But ere your labours for to-day are done,
> Two crystal slippers must be finely spun.

SILICA. Slippers of glass, why such were never seen;
> Surely two feel of glass requires our Queen.

CRYSTAL. Though shine they would without the aid of blacking,
> Glass slippers would be liable to cracking.

IRIS. Two crystal slippers are my special order,
> Made with a pretty ornamental border;
> Whoever then beholds them this will strike them,
> That nowhere in the world were slippers like them.

SILICA. The length?

IRIS. Same length as mine.

SILICA. Attend with pleasure,
> Two slippers—best material—fairy measure.

> *(Glass Goblins receive order, and signify readiness to execute it.)*

ALUMINA. Name and address of her for whom we make them?

SPARKLE. And see upon reflection, each best made is.
> Glass is so much looked into by the ladies.

IRIS. Endow them with a splendour most entrancing,
> Giving them ease, and elegance for dancing.

(ALUMINA advances with the pair of Glass Slippers made by the Goblins.)

ALUMINA. Behold the two glass slippers made have been,
Exactly to the orders of our Queen.

IRIS. This task accomplished every elf shall rest,
Well satisfied with having done his best;
A fitting wearer leave our Queen to find,
And show the purpose fairy powers designed.
Now is a dance of Crystal Chromatropes,
Let Iris see the promise of her hopes.

GRAND PRISMATIC BALLET

On which Scene closes.

SCENE III

Gardens of the Baron's Chateau.

Violent ringing of bells in every direction. Enter rapidly from opposite sides the two sisters, VIXENA the spiteful, and PAVONIA the proud. Each has a broken bell-rope in her hand, and both are furious with rage.

VIXENA. How water, Cinderella, will you bring it?
If I were near her nose, oh, wouldn't I wring it!

PAVONIA. Now, Cinderella, don't our ear me shouting?
Come, wash and comb my Poodle for his outing.

VIXENA. The tiresome hussy!

PAVONIA. Past all patience quite!

TOGETHER. Oh, here she comes at last! A pretty sight!

> *(Enter CINDERELLA as the poor kitchen drudge, with hearth-broom in one hand, and coal-scuttle in the other.)*

CINDERELLA. Here I am, sisters! What do you require?
I only stayed to make up kitchen fire.

PAVONIA. Make up indeed! Don't with the grate make free.

CINDERELLA. Yes you make up to every spark you see.

VIXENA. The kitchen fire wants little, I've no doubt.

CINDERELLA. Even a little always puts you out.
There don't be cross, you know how quick my aid'is;
I am the drudge while you are the fine ladies.

106

The hardest work I am not the girl to mind,
But from my kin I have words much less than kind;
A maid-of-all-work—deeply to be pitied,
No Sunday out—no followers permitted.

PAVONIA. And serve you right—it's as it ought to be,
You work because you are youngest of the three!

VIXENA. Of course. Because you have got a pretty face,
You mustn't be stuck up, but know your place.

CINDERELLA. And am I never to go out to parties,
And know what satisfaction a sweetheart is?

PAVONIA. Certainly not! You'll in the kitchen tarry
Until your elder sisters choose to marry.

CINDERELLA. Oh! for my duster to sop up my tears!
You won't get married for these many years.

Air—"Real Jam"

CINDERELLA and **SISTERS**.
THEY ARE/WE ARE REAL JAM! ALL JAM!
I'M ONLY/SHE'S ONLY SHAM, NOT WHAT I AM.

CINDERELLA.
REAL JAM! MAMMY, MAM, MAM!
OH, WHY WAS I YOUNGEST MADE?
THERE! DON'T BE CROSS!
LAST NIGHT I DREAMT!—BUT STAY
IT'S QUITE A PRETTY STORY IN ITS WAY.

Song—"Cinderella"

ONCE THERE LIVED A LITTLE MAIDEN,
SCORNED BY SISTERS, PERT AND PROUD;
WHILE WITH GRIEF HER HEART WAS LADEN,
THEY WOULD SEEK THE JOYOUS CROWD.
LEFT AT HOME, THE DAMSEL LONELY
BITTERLY WOULD WEEP HER WRONG,
AND FOR CONSOLATION ONLY
SAND SHE ONCE THIS SIMPLE SONG;--

"THERE MAY COME A DAY WHEN A PRINCE THIS WAY
MAY PASS WITH HIS COURTLY TRAIN,
AND FIND IN THIS PLACE THE KIND OF FACE
HE MAY WISH IN HIS HEART TO REMAIN."

NEVER HEED HOW OLD THE TELLING
OF THIS SIMPLY FAIRY TALE—
THERE MAY YET BE MANY A DWELLING
WHERE THE MORAL MAY AVAIL.
NOT TO THOSE WHO ARE ALWAYS STRIVING
MEN TO CATCH AND FORTUNES BRING
FALLS THE PRIZE, AT LAST ARRIVING
FOR ONE LEFT AT HOME TO SING—

THERE MAY COME A DAY WHEN A PRINCE THIS WAY
MAY PASS WITH A COURTLY TRAIN,
AND FIND A FACE IN THIS HUMBLE PLACE
HE WILL LONG IN HIS HEART RETAIN.

*(Rapid music. KOBOLD runs in with large bottle labelled
"Physic for the Baron." Shakes it up according to directions, and
then tries contents, found unpleasant to the palate.)*

KOBOLD. More physic for the Baron! "To be taken
Three times a day, the bottle being well shaken."
Rheumatic gout on poor old master seizes,
This comes of hunting boars and catching sneezes.

(Enter BARON, as invalid.)

BARON. Chasing the wild buck, following the boar,
Won't suit the Baron Pumpernickel more.
Though in my time I have made great bags of fame,
I give up being a sportsman all the same.

KOBOLD. Behond the draught.

BARON. *(Abstractedly.)* One million boars I have followed.

KOBOLD. The mixture as before. Thrice daily swallowed.

BARON. Throw doctors to the dogs—don't see the fun of 'em,
No, stop a little, save the dose for one of 'em.

CINDERELLA. Let me, Papa, prepare some savoury gruel.

PAVONIA. You wouldn't physic my poor dog, Pa! cruel!

VIXENA. The girl's quite bad enough to do things dreadful,
Or every wicked thought she has her head full.

BARON. That dreadful Poodle, girl, does things unlawful.
As for its goings on--it's something awful!

108

THERE WILL COME UPON MY TOES A THING ZOOLOGICAL,
THEN FLOP UPON MY NOSE IN A WAY ILLOGICAL.
IF HE HAD A BIOGRAPHER,
OR I WAS A TOPOGRAPHER,
I'LL HAVE HIM TAKEN OFF BY A CHEAP PHOTOGRAPHER.

(Trumpets without.)

BARON. Silence, attend! Some royal proclamation.

(Music. Enter Heralds, Guards, and the Prince's page BIZARRE, with large envelope. CINDERELLA kept in background with difficulty.)

BIZARRE. This from our prince. A card of invitation.
Grand Ball takes place this evening. Prince requests
The Baron's daughters as his royal guests.

BARON. We are highly honoured, and my daughters too!

BIZARRE. Three, Baron, are they not?

BARON. A pair will do.

(More difficulty with CINDERELLA.)

BIZARRE. Ladies of every, land are here invited.

BARON. I am sure my daughters will be both delighted.

BIZARRE. Beauties are always welcome beyound measure.

BARON. Thanks, we accept the offer with much pleasure.
(BARON takes BIZARRE aside.)
Go on, a purse of gold shall do thee good,
If things come off exactly as they should.
(March music resumed, and exeunt BIZARRE, HERALD, and Guards.)
Dear me! I feel in such a dreadful flurry!
About your dresses you will have to hurry.
Where's Cinderella? I will make the jade
Come and assist you as your waiting-maid.

CINDERELLA. And may I not like you attend the ball?

PAVONIA. Presumptuous minx!

VIXENA. I'd catch you there—that's all!
Come and try on our dresses. Thought entrancing!

BARON. For gout, they say, there's no such cure as dancing.

I'll trip upon the light fantastic tow,
And rid of gouty twinges get, just so.

(*BARON tries a few steps, when the objectionable Poodle enters
and worries him in a variety of ways. The BARONS's wrath at
last ungovernable, and he remonstrates with the Poodle in the
severest fashion.*)

CHORUS—OMNES
Air—"Run for the Doctor"

FUN FOR THE MOMENT, FATHER DEAR,
POODLE'S SHAKEN AWFULLY QUEER.
NONE FOR HIS LIFE, WOULD BITE OR SP
OFFER TO HIM IF HE DON'T GET UP.
PAT HIM UPON HIS LITTLE BACK,
OFFER HIM CAKES, AND NUTS TO CRACK.
PERSEVERE, OR HE WON'T, WE FEAR,
OPEN HIS EYES IN THE MORNING.

(*Poodle recovers under conciliatory treatment, and all dance off
to tune as Scene changes to*)

SCENE IV

The Kitchen in the Baronial Hall

*The kitchen well furnished. Large Fireplace. Spacious Dresser, Sink,
Ironing Board, etc. Doors on each side leading to the opposite room of
BARON and his two daughters. Pantomime Music. Enter rapidly the
sisters, VIXENA the spiteful, and PAVONIA the proud, followed by
CINDERELLA loaded with dresses thrown over her arm, and
overwhelmed with band-boxes.*

VIXENA. Now, Cinderella, see your hands are clean,
And bring my thingumies—you know what I mean.

PAVONIA. Where is my blue and silver? Go and see.
I shall expect you to attend on me.

VIXENIA. Come, do my hair in style that will surprise.

PAVONIA. Help me to dress, and fasten hooks and eyes.

CONDERELLA. One at a time, dear sisters. Understand,
I don't mind giving each a helping hand;
But as my arms are limited to two,
For both at once these hands will never do.

110

VIXENA. A hand a-place upon each ear be branded.
There's mine. *(Applied accordingly.)*

PAVONIA. And mine. (Action repeated.)

CINDERELLA. Two fishing smacks just landed.
But still both ears, though boxed with all your heart,
You ought to know will only make me smart.

SISTERS. Peace!

CINDERELLA. Yes! Each sister, being of blows a donor,
Leaves me no peace until she finds much on her.

DUET—SISTERS
Air—"I'll Beat You More for That Than Anything"

WE'LL TREAT YOU WORSE THAN THAT IF ANYTHING;
IF A BOY YOUR SISTERS HAD,
WE'D BEAT HIM MORE FOR THAT THAN ANYTHING.
ISN'T SHE DREADFUL? ISN'T SHE BAD?

Solo—CINDERELLA—Same Air repeated.

THEY TREAT ME, I MAY SAY, LIKE ANYTHING,
NOT A JOY I'VE EVER HAD,
DON'T TREAT ME EVEN TO A PENNY THING.
ISN'T IT SHAMEFUL? ISN'T IS SAD?

(Enter BARON with appeared on his arm.)

BARON. Now, girls, girls, girls, make haste, we shall be late;
Our carriages are ordered round at eight.
(Flurry of the Sisters.)
Both go and dress, I'll have a wash up here.
Over your Poodle I've went tears sincere.

PAVONIA. Our pretty Poppett?

(BARON impatient.)

VIXENA. La! Pa! How you hurry one!

BARON. Thank goodness, there's no Poodle left to worry one.

PAVONIA. Now, Cinderella, come--but keep your distance.

BARON. My kitchen dresser must give me assistance.

VIXENA. Assist her first. Although I now am dumb,
I'll be revenged! my turn has yet to come.

(Exit in a rage.)

CINDERELLA. Oh! what a life! all pummelling and pushing.
I have got more pins stuck in me than their "cushing."

(PAVONIA pushes CINDERELLA before her, through door.)

BARON. The Poodle's settled, of all comfort greatest,
Now at the Ball we mustn't be the latest.
That rascal! Kobold I'll dismiss next quarter,
Why don't he bring me the hot shaving water?

(Enter KOBOLD with hot water, ad BARON begins his preparations for the Ball. The objectionable Poodle comes silly on, and causes BARON great discomfiture by running away with various articles of apparel, the suspicion of all misadventures being directed towards DOBOLD. Dog finally disposed of in a copper.)

BARON. Delicious waltzes wander through my brain,
I feel in fancy quite a youth again.

(Baron's reminiscence of Waltz tunes, blended occasionally with modern Music Hall airs.)

Air—*"Bloomsbury Square"*

Brush up my hair! Comb it out fair,
Find out a place for a parting up there.
Mind you take care, you will know where
The division should be when you brush up my hair.
Air--'The Merry Chink, Chink, Chink"
Oh, I'll give to every lady such a wink, wink, wink!
I'm a Don Giovanni they will think, think, think;
They will say "Upon my life, of politeness you're the pink,
Oh, never gave a Baron such a wink, wink, wink!"

(BARON now equipped for the Ball.)

Ladies may enter--daughters, see your Pa!
The paragon of elegance--comme ca.

(VIXENA and PAVONIA enter in Ball-room dress.)

VIXENA. Now, Cinderella, I'm not half done yet.

PAVONIA. Another turn I want, you quite forget.

(CINDERELLA enters, pushing on large toilet-table with large looking-glass and box upon it, etc.)

CINDERELLA. There, help yourselves, much uglier I have seen you
But make up pretty, if you can, between you.

(Toilet-table now in centre.)

PAVONIA. Here, dress my hair in most becoming style.

VIXENA. Arrange my ringlets, these things look most vile.

> *(Music. Business of toilet. CINDERELLA and Sisters. The BARON and KOBOLD criticizing the result after their own fashion.)*

PAONIA. A longer run no one shall have me,
This curtset Pa's worth a Diploma see?

> *(Acting accordingly, corrected by BARON. VIXENA unobserved goes to the table where PAVONIA'S card of invitation, etc., has been placed in a box. VIXENA cautiously approaches the box, showing suppressed manganite a la Zioka in "Diplomacy.")*

VIXENA. I've seen a play in which they called a speaker
Who searched for everything, the Countess Seeker.
> *(Melodramatic Music.)*
Pavonia's baulked my will, I'll make her rue it.
Let's see! I'll steak her program. Yes! I'll do it.
She'll suspect Cinder! Oh, it will be fun—
No one is looking. One, two, three, it's done.

> *(VIXENA turns key and abstracts paper.)*

BARON. Now to the Prince's Ball. Come, girls, you'll do.

CINDERELLA. How I should like to go! Please let me.

BARON. Pooh!
Do you think such folks would find a slut bewitchen'?
Keep company with the grate that's in the kitchen.
We shall be home by midnight—not before,
Don't dare to keep up waiting at the door.

> *(Descriptive Music. CINDERELLA makes an ineffectual entreaty to accompany the Party, seconded by KOBOLD, who thereupon gets sharply rebuffed by BARON. The other Sisters ridicule the notion, and go off tauntingly, followed by the BARON with dignity, grotesquely imitated by KOBOLD, who follows in attendance.)*

CINDERELLA.
They are gone, and here must Cinderella stay,
Passing long hours dreamingly away.
Kept thus at home, no wonder I feel lonely,
Here if I stir, it's with the poker only;
I see no form my face to inspire,

No faces but the faces in the fire.
Wild thoughts my bright imagination fills,
Let's have the "Lancers," first set of Quadrilled.

(Arranged mops and brooms for partners.)

DANCING SONG
Air—"First Figure of the Lancers"

NOW FIRST YOU SET TO ME,
AND THEN I SET TO YOU,
AND THEN WE TURN EACH OTHER ABOUT,
AND, THANK YOU, THAT WILL DO.
THE MOP SHOULD BE ADVANCING,
AND GO LEADING ON THE BROOM,
THEN OFF WE ALL GO DANCING
WITH OUR PARTNERS ROUND THE ROOM.
AND THEN YOU SET TO ME,
AND THEN I SET TO YOU,
AND THEN WE TURN EACH OTHER ABOUT,
AND, THANK YOU, THAT WILL DO.

(Ball-room music and picture of dancers seen in grate.)

CINDERELLA. Good gracious, that's the very situation,
But how absurd! It's all imagination.

(Figures disappear and Fairy IRIS becomes visible.)

IRIS. Not so my child they real shall appear.
I was your Fairy Godmother, my dear!
I know your wishes, and will grant them all.
First you would like to see the Prince's Ball.
(CINDERELLA is delighted, but points to her attire.)
Don't be alarmed, I can your meaning guess-
You wouldn't like to go in such a dress;
I'll see to that.

CINDERELLA. Oh! thank you, ma'am, how kind!

(KOBOLD rushes in.)

IRIS. You would go, too! a place for you I'll find—
To follow and to wait upon her leisure.
See, I can fit you both without a measure.

*(CINDERELLA appears with her Opera Cloak, and KOBOLD
handsomely equipped.)*

Now for your Coach! From garden wall behind,

Bring me the largest Pumpkin you can find.

(KOBOLD brings Pumpkin.)

So, place it there. I want now some White Mice:
These I will turn to Ponies in a trice.

(KOBOLD places trap of White Mice on dresser.)

Now we a whiskered Coachman must provide.
Bring yonder trap—a fie large Rat's inside.

(Rat trap brought by KOBOLD.)

Now for some Lizards--there are surely lots
About the garden, near those flower-pots.

(KOBOLD brings Lizards in flower-pots.)

The very things for Footmen these will be.
And now prepare to see what you shall see!

(IRIS touches the various articles, and CINDERELLA'S Carriage is produced, with Coachman, Foomen, etc.)

Isn't that grand? Oh, stop a Cabbage pray.

(KOBOLD produces Cabbage.)

This I transform into a fine bouquet.

(Change accordingly.)

Two Slippers made of glass I give you.

CINDERELLA. Oh! I must look dazzling now from top to toe.

(CINDERELLA receives her Glass Slippers, and expresses her delight and gratitude.)

IRIS. Remember this! past midnight if you stay,
Coach, Coachman, Footmen, all will run away.

SONG—CINDERELLA
Air—"Gallop from Gustavus 3rd"

I'M OFF TO THE BALL, WHICH SOME MAY CALL
A GREAT ADVANCE FROM THE SERVANTS' HALL;
BUT STILL I KNOW FROM THE SERVANTS' HALL;
BUT STILL I KNOW I'M TREATED SO,
BECAUSE THEY WANT ME KEPT BELOW.
OH, WHAT DANCING, JOY ENTRANCING,
SHALL WE HAVE WHEN THERE WE GO!
CARRIAGE READY, COACHMAN STEADY,

ISN'T IT DELIGHTFUL, OH!
I'M OFF TO THE BALL, ETC.

(Scene closing on Tableau.)

SCENE V

Corridor in the Prince's Palace.

Lively Music. Loud rapping at doors, and ringing of bells, as visitors arrive in succession. Enter WISEWITZ, the Tutor of Prince, with BIZARRE the Page, Chamberlain, the Two Heralds, and Attendants. WISEWITZ marshals them in proper order.

WISE. Each like a preposition, go before,
Preceding those who are knocking more and more.
All to your various posts at once away.
Bizarre the page will in the lobby stay.

> *(Tremendous knocking and ringing. Distinguished guests arrive and are ceremoniously conducted across.)*

All the wax candles brilliantly are lighted,
All have accepted who have been invited.

> *(Knock! Ring! More visitors cross, followed by Attendants as before.)*

The best of bands! Our orchestra's immense,
All are engaged regardless of expense.

> *(More knocking and ringing. Visitors cross, preceded by Heralds, Chamberlain, and Attendants as before.)*

Yet if the Prince finds none his dream to match,
He gives a ball with nobody to catch.

> *(Peculiarly prolonged knock and eccentric ring. Enter BARON with his two daughters PAVONIA and VIXENA, preceded by the Heralds, Chamberlain, and Attendants as before. The Sisters, mistaking the Attendants for visitors, salute them cordially, and are corrected by the BARON accordingly.)*

BARON. Now, girls, just look as handsome as you can.
I really feel I'm quite a ladies' man.
(Pompously.) What sort of people have you here to-day?

WISE. All pronouns I, She, He, Me, You, and They.

BARON. I'm Baron Pumpernickel of renown,
We wanted to inquire what names were down.

WISE. A noun to answer an inquiry right so
  Must be in the same case with--

BARON. Just so! Quite so!
  (Aside.) I know to e'en the primest of prime ministers
  A grateful country some reward administers.
  Where is my purse? From place to place I've followed it.
  Why, that confounded Poodle's been and swallowed it.

PAVONIA. My beauty, Pa, I know will be sufficient.

VIXENA. Beauty! The gift in which she's quite deficient.

  *(Rivalry of the Sisters in playing off their attractions on the Tutor.
  BARON still fumbling for a coin in vain.)*

BARON. No matter, if to-night a lucky suitor,
  I may have sons, and you shall be their tutor.

Air—"Pretty Polly Pouter"

BARON, VIXENA, PAVONIA.
  JUST SO—ON WE GO—BARON IS A RUM ONE, OH!
  WE'RE MAD WITH GLEE, FOR ALL THE THREE
  ARE BENT UPON MARRYING SOME ONE, OH!

Air—"The Runaway Musketeer"

  POINT YOUR TOES, AND RAISE YOUR THUMBS,
  SHOW US THE WAY THE NOBILITY COMES;
  THE WORD OF A WHISPER IN MY EAR
  WILL BE GOOD FOR A RUNAWAY MATCH THIS YEAR.

  (OMNES dancing off.)

SCENE VI

The Illuminated Ball Room.

*Clock marking the hour of "Eleven." All the visitors discovered. Dance
commences the scene; when dance is over, enter PRINCE, Page and
Attendants. PRINCE obtrusively followed by BARON and his two
daughters, who are being perpetually introduced, and who are, to the
BARONS' discomfiture, continually discarded. BARON puts them in the
most prominent positions to attract notice, and while refreshments are
being handed round, consumes them largely, and proceeds to flirt on his
own account. WIZEWITZ the Tutor ceremoniously officiating.*

PRINCE. Alas! not here! I vainly look around,

Her charming feature nowhere can be found.

(BIZARRE the Page comes forward.)

BIZARRE. Sire! There is just arrived a great princess,
Of name unknown, but lovely to excess.

PRINCE. Can this be her? 'Tis strange no name to mention.
Go, pay her every possible attention.

(Marked Music. BIZARRE goes off, and returns ceremoniously with CINDERELLA who arrives KOBODL in attendance. The PRINCE recognizes and receives her with great delight. Varied effect upon the Guests.)

PRINCE. Beyound my hopes of happiness, 'tis she!
Beauteous Princess, my heart is given to thee.

CINDERELLA. Isn't this nice? You must excuse, your highness,
If this great shine creates a little shyness.

PRINCE. Fear noting! Take my arm and let us chat.

CINDERELLA. There cannot be a deal of harm in that.

PRINCE. Oh, thank of one!

CINDERELLA. You give me quite a shock.
I really must be home by twelve o'clock.

(PRINCE and CINDERELLA seated, and deeply engaged in conversation. Refreshments liberally handed round to the Visitors, CINDERELLA being always intercepted with the trays of Negus, Sandwiches, etc. to which KOBOLD and BARON earnestly devote themselves. PAVONIA and VIXENA in front of stage on opposite sides, endeavouring to attract attention of male visitors. Melodramatic Music. Sudden discovery of the resemblance of the new comers to CINDERELLA and KOBOLD. BARON brought down to centre.)

BARON. Good gracious! Gracious goodness! Goodness gra—

VIXENA and **PAVONIA**. Why what's the matter, Pa?

BARON. Look there!

VIXENA and **PAVONIA**. Which way?

(BARON points to new arrivals.)

BARON. How like to Cinderella!

PAVONIA. Did you ever?

VIXENA. Emphatically, I may say, I never.

(CINDERELLA, nervously reminded by KOBOLD of the progress of the house as indicated by clock now marking "Half-past Eleven.")

CINDERELLA. Half-past eleven! How the time does fly!

PRINCE. It always does when those we love are by.
But still the night is young. One moment hear me.

CINDERELLA. I feel such happiness when you are near me.

(CINDERELLA and PRINCE advances, BARON and his daughters observing at back.)

DUET
Air—"Blue and White Polka"

PRINCE.
COME, MY DARLING, KISS ME, KISS ME HERE.

CINDERELLA.
IF I WERE TO GO WOULD YOU MISS ME HERE?

PRINCE.
JOY IN MY HEART WOULD NEVERMORE BE.

CINDERELLA.
THEN KISS ME, BUT PLEASE DON'T LET ANYONE SEE.

(Repeat ad libitum.)

Quintette—Air—"Grandfather's Clock"

BARON, **PAVONIA**, **VIXENA**, and **KOBOLD.**
OH, LOOK AT THE CLOCK, HOW IT GOES ON TO TWELVES,
AS IT'S GONE MANY NIGHTS LONG BEFORE.
ALL GOOD PEOPLE, WE'RE TOLD, SHOULD TAKE CARE OF
    THEMSELVES,
AS THE WORLD DON'T CONTAIN ANY MORE.
IT IS NEARLY THE MORN, AND THE DEWS OF THE DAWN,
WHICH ARE DAMP, AND UNPLEASANT BESIDE,
BRING A THOUGHT—OUGHT WE EVER TO GO AGAIN
WHERE WE HOME CAN'T RIDE?
NOT A CAB WITHOUT STUMBLING, WHIP, WHIP, WHIP,
A RUDE CABBY GRAUMBLING, TIP, TIP, TIP,
AND WE'RE DROPPED SHORT SEVERAL STREET AGAIN
FROM—WHERE—WE—RE—SIDE.

(Chorus repeated.)

WISE. Now choose your partners for the first quadrille.

PRINCE. *(To CINDERELLA.)* I have chosen mine for life, if so you will.

BIZARRE. Highness will be pleased to have a dance.
Side couples take your places, top advance.

> *(Dance, through which runs operatic air.)*

CINDERELLA. I must fly, the time remember,
See how swiftly minutes pass!

PRINCE. Does there come the sad farewell then?
Saddest hour of all, alas!

> *(Clock strikes Twelve, and in the midst of the dance CINDERELLA rushes away, leaving the Glass Slipper found by PRINCE. Consternation of everybody, and BARON's daughters fainting into everybody's arms. Scene closed in by)*

SCENE VII

The En-Corridor—By General Request

Rapid Music. Flight of male attendants across stage is search of CINDERELLA. Enter PRINCE with Glass Slipped, Page ad Heralds.

PRINCE. Through all my kingdom let this news be rife,
Who owns the slipper I shall own my wife.
Go forth, my Heralds. Through the land proclaim it,
And for reward you only have to name it.

> *(Exit PRINCE and Heralds. Enter BARON PUMPERNICKEL, visible affected by what he has taken, KOBOLD endeavoring to make him preserve the perpendicular, and anxious to avoid being recognized.)*

BARON. Find some conveyance quickly for the pair;
I rather think to-night I was all there.
How soon ham sandwiches get in one's head.

> *(Enter PAVONIA and VIXENA.)*

VIXENA. Papa! It's time we got you home to bed.

PAVONIA. Two cavaliers have very kindly proffered
To see us home, and their sedans have offered.

BARON. All right, my dears. I'll go and see about them.
One toast, "The ladies," couldn't live without them.

(Exeunt BARON and KOBOLD. Rapid music. Male guests enter, and cross. Business. The two sisters struggling to find an eligible escort. At last satisfied, and all go off. Scene discovering)

SCENE VIII

Courtyard of the Baron's Mansion.

Snowy morning. CHANTICLER, the Watchman, enters crosses stage. "Past two o'clock, and a snowy morning," goes off. Enter CINDERELLA, half changed from her ball-room attire from side, and falls on steps of door, after the style of "Jane Shore" in Mr. Wills' popular play.

CINDERELLA. I have had no supper! Dreams of joy I cherish,
But none of food. I starve! Don't hear! I perish!
Where am I? On the steps I've cleaned, but look,
How different from the steps last night I took.
Ah, this is as the Fairy said it would be,
If not returning at the time I should be.

GRAND SCENA—CINDERELLA
Air—"The Blue Alsatian Mountains"

GIRLS FOR INFORMATION SEEKING
OF A PRINCE WHO'S YOUNG AND FAIR,
LIKE THE ONE OF WHOM I'M SPEAKING,
YOU HAD BETTER NOW TAKE CARE.
HE HAS BEEN AFFECTION WINNING,
HE DID MY POOR HEART BEGUILE
TALES OF LOVE SO QUICKLY SPINNING;
I COULD ONLY SAY THE WHILE
HEYDAY! HEYDAY! HEYDAY!
SUCH WORDS WILL PASS AWAY,
THOUGH HIS TALES OF LOVE RECOUNTING
SEEM BUT WHISPERED YESTERDAY.

(Opens door with latch-key and goes in. Enter PAVONIA and VIXENA with large umbrellas, and in pattens.)

PAVONIA. If this is going to a Prince's Ball,
I'm sure must rather I had not gone at all.

VIXENA. Well, certainly we don't look quite bewitchin'
But let's go in. This bell rings in the kitchen.

(Pulls bell. Sound heard.)

PAVONIA. And Cinderella must be sitting up,
At all events we have had a dance and sup.

(Door opened, and they enter. Music. BARON and KOBOLD brought home in sedan chairs. Men require money. BARON very inebriated.)

BARON. I have nothing but a cheque. Half-crown for rounds,
Give me the difference for a hundred pounds.

(Men take poles away, and go off threatening a summary process.)

BARON. I don't know who you are that came with me,
But this is fun, I think. Don't you agree?
Didn't that Countess say, "My love without it—"
I'm a gay fellow. There's no doubt about it.
Now let's see. Fellows, open the sedan!
When there's no fellows--don't see how they can.

(Music. Much difficulty in extricating themselves from sedan, by which time, bright morning, and stage light. Trumpet heard. March, and enter WISEWITZ, BIZARRE, Heralds, Chamberlains, and Guards.)

WISE. Whereas last night.

BIZARRE. A lady at the ball.

WISE. Dropped a glass slipper.

BIZARRE. Very neat and small.

WISE. This is to state to all throughout the land,
Who shows the foot shall have the Prince's hand.

(PAVONIA and VIXENA appear at door.)

BARON. Come, girls, the Prince will here his hand bestow.
One's sure to put her foot in it I know.
That comes to pass which I so long foresaw,
The Prince will be my Royal son-in-law.

(Enter CINDERELLA from door, and confers with KOBOLD.)

CINDERELLA. That slipper, Kobold, must be mine I know;
One I found left, the Prince my right can show.
I think I stand a chance to get a place
Among the foremost in this great foot-race.

(Enter PRINCE and attendants. One bearing glass slipper on crimson cushion.)

PRINCE. Here is the slipper! None shall have denial,

Though all in vain I know will be the trial,
By not one here can this small feat be done.

(WISEWITZ places stool and slipper. Female competitors appear. Trial rapidly made.)

PRINCE. What's the result?

WISE. A failure every one.

PRINCE. I thought as much, who's next?

(BARON, VIXENA, and PAVONIA advance.)

BARON. Now which declares it,
Where the shoe pinches, she but knows who wears it.

(PAVONIA tries.)

There, nearly on! We couldn't get the heel in.

(VIXENA tries.)

A perfect fit, she's gone into with kneelin'.

(PRINCE discovers CINDERELLA.)

PRINCE. This humble maiden--let her try for one.

(All eagerly, but incredulously, KOBOLD excepted, watch the trial. PRINCE much interested.)

PRINCE. It looks the size—it is—it's on—it's done!
You are—!

CINDERELLA. I am!

PRINCE. If so, then you must be,
The fair princess—

CINDERELLA. And so I was.

PRINCE. *(Embracing her.)* 'Tis she!

(Enter IRIS.)

IRIS. Cease your surprise. A Fairy in reality,
I have taught this girl the need of punctuality.
Henceforth young ladies who her fate behold,
Will come from balls the moment they are told.

CINDERELLA. That hours pass swiftly every one agrees;
We hope that nothing "slow" you have found in these.
Our general joy may each one here be sharing,
And our Glass Slipper turn out good for wearing.

GRAND PAS FANTASTIQUE

THUS OUR DAYS WILL MERRILY END,
IF WE FIND WITH EACH A FRIEND.
MAY THE DAYS THAT BRING US PEACE
EVERY FIND OUR FRIENDS INCREASE.

THE TRANSFORMATION

Harlequinade Commences

E N D

Manufactured by Amazon.ca
Bolton, ON

30759665R00070